TRANSPORTATION INFRASTRUCTURE -
ROADS, HIGHWAYS, BRIDGES, AIRPORTS AND MASS TRANSIT

MILLENNIUM CHALLENGE CORPORATION

TRANSPORTATION INFRASTRUCTURE PROJECT RESULTS

Transportation Infrastructure - Roads, Highways, Bridges, Airports and Mass Transit

Additional books in this series can be found on Nova's website under the Series tab.

Additional E-books in this series can be found on Nova's website under the E-book tab.

TRANSPORTATION INFRASTRUCTURE -
ROADS, HIGHWAYS, BRIDGES, AIRPORTS AND MASS TRANSIT

MILLENNIUM CHALLENGE CORPORATION

TRANSPORTATION INFRASTRUCTURE PROJECT RESULTS

JUSTIN LANE
AND
JOSEPH DUNN
EDITORS

nova publishers
New York

For permission to use material from this book please contact us:
Telephone 631-231-7269; Fax 631-231-8175
Web Site: http://www.novapublishers.com

Library of Congress Cataloging-in-Publication Data

ISBN: 978-1-62808-184-8

Published by Nova Science Publishers, Inc. † New York

CONTENTS

PREFACE

The Millennium Challenge Corporation (MCC), is a U.S. government corporation, which was established in 2004 to provide aid to developing countries that have demonstrated a commitment to ruling justly, encouraging economic freedom, and investing in people. To help developing countries reduce poverty and stimulate economic growth, the MCC has approved 26 bilateral compact agreements totaling about $9.3 billion. In the seven compacts that ended in 2010 and 2011, Honduras, Cape Verde, Nicaragua, Vauatu, Georgia, Armenia, and Benin; transportation infrastructure projects generally received about 50 percent of the compact's total funding. To measure the results of its compacts, MCC sets targets for various performance indicators, such as number of kilometers paved or volume of merchandise passing through a port, and estimates the number of beneficiaries. This book examines the extent to which MCC has, for transportation infrastructure projects, achieved expected performance targets, and consistently estimated the numbers of beneficiaries.

Chapter 1 - To help developing countries reduce poverty and stimulate economic growth, MCC has approved 26 bilateral compact agreements totaling about $9.3 billion. In the seven compacts that ended in 2010 and 2011—Honduras, Cape Verde, Nicaragua, Vanuatu, Georgia, Armenia, and Benin— transportation infrastructure projects generally received about 50 percent of the compact's total funding. To measure the results of its compacts, MCC sets targets for various performance indicators—such as number of kilometers paved or volume of merchandise passing through a port—and estimates the number of beneficiaries. This report, responding to a congressional mandate, examines the extent to which MCC has, for transportation infrastructure projects, (1) achieved expected performance targets and (2) consistently estimated numbers of beneficiaries. GAO analyzed MCC documents, interviewed MCC officials, and drew on fieldwork completed for related work in four of the seven countries.

Chapter 2 - MCC was established in 2004 to help developing countries reduce poverty and stimulate economic growth through multiyear compact agreements. As of June 2012, MCC had signed 26 compacts totaling about $9.3 billion in assistance. Seven compacts, including those with Georgia and Benin, closed in 2010 or 2011. Most had a transportation infrastructure project (a road or a port) that received about 50 percent of the compact's total funding. This report, prepared in response to a congressional mandate to review compact results, examines how MCC ensured the quality and sustainability of MCC's two transportation infrastructure projects in Georgia and Benin. GAO analyzed MCC documents, interviewed MCC officials and stakeholders, and observed the transportation infrastructure projects in those countries.

In: Millennium Challenge Corporation
Editors: Justin Lane and Joseph Dunn
ISBN: 978-1-62808-184-8

Chapter 1

MILLENNIUM CHALLENGE CORPORATION: RESULTS OF TRANSPORTATION INFRASTRUCTURE PROJECTS IN SEVEN COUNTRIES*

United States Government Accountability Office

WHY GAO DID THIS STUDY

To help developing countries reduce poverty and stimulate economic growth, MCC has approved 26 bilateral compact agreements totaling about $9.3 billion. In the seven compacts that ended in 2010 and 2011—Honduras, Cape Verde, Nicaragua, Vanuatu, Georgia, Armenia, and Benin—transportation infrastructure projects generally received about 50 percent of the compact's total funding. To measure the results of its compacts, MCC sets targets for various performance indicators—such as number of kilometers paved or volume of merchandise passing through a port—and estimates the number of beneficiaries. This report, responding to a congressional mandate, examines the extent to which MCC has, for transportation infrastructure projects, (1) achieved expected performance targets and (2) consistently estimated numbers of beneficiaries. GAO analyzed MCC documents,

* This is an edited, reformatted and augmented version of United States Government Accountability Office, Publication No. GAO-12-631, dated September 2012.

interviewed MCC officials, and drew on fieldwork completed for related work in four of the seven countries.

WHAT GAO RECOMMENDS

MCC should strengthen existing policies and practices regarding measuring and evaluating results data and formalize a quality review process to improve its beneficiary calculations. MCC agreed with all of our recommendations and outlined some steps the agency will take or has already taken to address them.

WHAT GAO FOUND

The Millennium Challenge Corporation (MCC)—a U.S. government corporation— recognizes the importance of a disciplined, transparent, and accountable approach to tracking compact results. However, it reduced the scopes of its early transportation infrastructure projects and reports mixed success in meeting key performance targets. In addition, problems with data quality call into question the reliability of those reported results. GAO found the following for the seven compacts ending in 2010 and 2011, each with a road project or a port project.

Road Projects

- MCC reduced kilometers to be paved under six compacts—Honduras, Cape Verde, Nicaragua, Vanuatu, Georgia, and Armenia—by a combined 63 percent (from about 1,800 to 600 km) because of increased construction costs and political problems in partner governments. MCC reported meeting reduced targets for five compacts. However, for three compacts, MCC did not consistently account for kilometers completed with funding from third parties.
- MCC reported meeting revised targets for road roughness—a measure of pavement quality—for five of the compacts. However, reported data have quality issues, including the inconsistent application of measurement methodologies and calculation errors that resulted in overstated results.

- MCC reported meeting targets for annual average daily traffic—a measure of the volume of traffic using the road—for three of the compacts. However, weaknesses in traffic baseline estimates may have affected the establishment of targets and therefore MCC's ability to measure results.

Port Projects

- In Cape Verde, MCC funding ($53.7 million) was insufficient to construct all planned port elements. As a result, MCC reduced the project's scope and deferred measuring the results of key indicators.
- In Benin, MCC completed most of the envisioned scope of the port project. MCC's data show that the compact met the original target for one of three key performance indicators, volume of merchandise. (The other two indicators relate to the measurement of shipping costs.) However, GAO found that MCC's estimation of this indicator's baseline may lead to overstated results. In addition, data quality reviews identified problems with the data used, which MCA-Benin did not formally address.

In 2009, MCC improved its methodology for estimating beneficiaries—people who realize income gains or expenditure savings as a result of its investment— by standardizing its approach. MCC subsequently revised its beneficiary numbers for all compacts. However, the new approach did not include a formal quality review process. As a result, implementation of the new approach suffered from varying degrees of quality problems. For example, (1) MCC did not implement its beneficiary estimation methodology consistently across early transportation infrastructure projects; (2) beneficiary calculations contained incorrect formulas and numbers, and differed from supporting documents; and (3) beneficiary figures in MCC's public documents were sometimes inaccurate.

ABBREVIATIONS

IRI	International Roughness Index
MCC	Millennium Challenge Corporation
MCA	Millennium Challenge Account

September 12, 2012

The Honorable Patrick Leahy
Chairman

The Honorable Lindsey Graham
Ranking Member
Subcommittee on the Department of State,
Foreign Operations, and Related Programs
Committee on Appropriations
United States Senate

The Honorable Kay Granger
Chairwoman

The Honorable Nita Lowey
Ranking Member
Subcommittee on State, Foreign Operations, and
Related Programs
Committee on Appropriations
House of Representatives

The Millennium Challenge Corporation (MCC), a U.S. government corporation, was established in 2004 to provide aid to developing countries that have demonstrated a commitment to ruling justly, encouraging economic freedom, and investing in people. MCC provides assistance to eligible countries through multiyear compact agreements to fund specific projects aimed at reducing poverty and stimulating economic growth. MCC's core principles include assessing the results of its funding to determine how its activities affect poverty and economic growth. To do this, MCC has instituted a monitoring and evaluation approach that includes identifying relevant indicators to measure results during and at the end of project implementation and establishing performance targets for each indicator. MCC's efforts to determine how its activities will affect poverty and economic growth also include estimating the number of people who will benefit from its projects and analyzing the impact of its projects on populations of specific interest.

As of June 2012, MCC had signed 26 compacts, committing a total of approximately $9.3 billion.[1] Seven of these compacts ended in 2010 or 2011:

Honduras, Cape Verde, Nicaragua, Vanuatu, Georgia, Armenia, and Benin.[2] (See app. II for compact time frames.)

In the fiscal year 2008 Consolidated Appropriations Act, Congress mandated that we review the results achieved by MCC compacts. [3] We have previously reported on the results of MCC's transportation infrastructure projects in four countries. In July 2011, we reported that MCC had met reduced targets for its compacts with Cape Verde and Honduras, the first two compacts to reach completion.[4] In June 2012, we reported that MCC transportation infrastructure projects in Georgia and Benin varied in quality and may not be sustainable.[5] Because much of MCC's funding for compacts that ended in 2010 and 2011 focused on transportation infrastructure projects, this report examines the extent to which MCC has, for transportation infrastructure projects, (1) achieved expected performance targets and (2) used a consistent methodology to estimate numbers of beneficiaries.

To assess the extent to which MCC has achieved its performance targets for transportation infrastructure projects under compacts that ended in 2010 and 2011, we reviewed MCC guidance and policy documents and analyzed compact agreements, monitoring and evaluation plans, and results data. We compared actual results achieved at the end of the compact for select performance indicators with MCC's original targets and, in some cases, with revised targets associated with each indicator. Since MCC tracks many performance indicators for each compact project, we selected a subset of indicators to examine for this report.

- For the road projects, we examined kilometers of road completed, roughness as a measure of road quality, and average annual daily traffic. We selected those road project indicators because they address the projects' key objectives and because they are among the "common indicators" MCC requires for all road projects, so that it can aggregate results across countries.
- For the port projects, we examined the volume of merchandise through the port and two indicators related to the measurement of shipping costs: container ship time at berth and container ship time at anchor. Because MCC has not established common indicators for ports, we selected indicators that addressed the projects' key objectives, corresponded to the common road indicators, and were originally included in both port projects.

Additionally, we interviewed MCC officials about data quality and indicator tracking tables. As part of our related engagements—focused on Cape Verde and Honduras, and on Georgia and Benin[6]—we visited compact projects in-country and met with partner country government officials, including those responsible for compact implementation, and with contractors, project managers, construction supervisors, and relevant private businesses.

To assess the extent to which MCC has consistently applied its beneficiary estimation methodology, we reviewed MCC's *Guidelines for Economic and Beneficiary Analysis* as well as its beneficiary calculations and accompanying supporting documents for the seven compacts that ended in 2010 and 2011. We compared original and revised beneficiary estimates for the transportation projects and assessed the justification behind any changes. Data are considered reliable when they are accurate, complete, consistent, and valid, given the uses for which they are intended. MCC enters into a legal relationship with partner country governments that vest an accountable entity with responsibility for day-to-day management of compact project implementation, including monitoring and evaluation activities such as setting and revising performance targets. Because such actions require MCC's direct oversight and approval, throughout this report, we attribute all decisions related to project rescoping and compact targets to MCC. (See app. I for further details of our objectives, scope, and methodology.) We conducted this performance audit from August 2011 to September 2012, as part of a body of work on this subject, in accordance with generally accepted government auditing standards. Those standards require that we plan and perform the audit to obtain sufficient, appropriate evidence to provide a reasonable basis for our findings and conclusions based on our audit objectives. We believe the evidence obtained provides a reasonable basis for our findings and conclusions based on our audit objectives.

BACKGROUND

MCC Organization

MCC is managed by a chief executive officer, appointed by the President with the advice and consent of the Senate, and is overseen by a Board of Directors. The Secretary of State serves as board chair and the Secretary of the Treasury as vice-chair.[7] MCC's model of providing foreign aid is based on a set of core principles deemed essential for effective development assistance, including good governance, country ownership, focus on results, and transparency. According to MCC, country ownership of an MCC compact occurs when a country's national government controls the prioritization process during compact development, is responsible for implementation, and is accountable to its domestic stakeholders for decision making and results. To implement the compact, the partner government establishes an accountable entity, referred to as a Millennium Challenge Account (MCA).[8] MCC provides the framework and guidance for compact implementation, monitoring, and evaluation that MCAs are to use in implementing compact projects.

Transportation Infrastructure Projects

The seven MCC compacts completed in 2010 and 2011 each included a transportation infrastructure project that—except in the case of Armenia—received 50 percent or more of the compact's total funding (see fig.1).

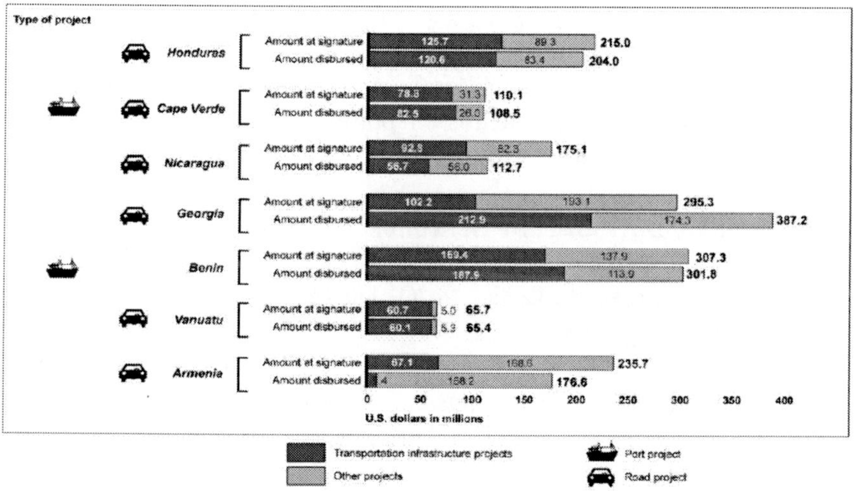

Source: GAO analysis of MCC data, Art Explosion (clip art).

Notes: Amount at signature is the amount allocated when MCC and the partner country sign the compact; amount disbursed is the actual amount disbursed by compact closure. Any undisbursed funds are returned to MCC. "Other projects" includes funds disbursed before the compact's entry into force, to facilitate implementation of the compact.

Figure 1. Funds for Transportation Infrastructure and Other Projects, by MCC Compact.

For the purposes of this report, we have defined transportation infrastructure as public works that convey passengers or goods from one place to another; infrastructure includes structures such as roads, seaports, airports, and railways. We reviewed five compacts with road projects, one with a port project, and one with both types of projects.

MCC Monitoring and Evaluation Framework

According to MCC's *Policy for Monitoring and Evaluation of Compacts and Threshold Programs*,[9] performance monitoring helps track progress toward compact goals and objectives and serves as a management tool. Therefore, MCC requires partner countries to create a monitoring and evaluation plan that they update throughout the course of the compact. The plan's monitoring component outlines the performance indicators by which the compact results will be measured. It also establishes a performance target for each indicator, including a baseline value (the starting value of an indicator) and the expected year by which the target will be achieved.[10] For some indicators, baseline measurements are necessary to establish interim and final targets. MCC and the MCAs monitor the progress of compact activities using an indicator tracking table, which is a reporting tool that displays targets and tracks progress against them. (See fig. 2.)

Transportation Infrastructure Indicators

MCC established common indicators in 2009 to aggregate results across countries.[11] For road projects, MCC has established several common indicators, including the following:[12]

- *Kilometers of road completed:* A measure of the total length of road completed under a compact. This indicator is a cumulative measure of works completed.
- *Road roughness*: A measure of pavement quality that affects ride quality, vehicle delay costs, fuel consumption, and maintenance costs. Roughness is used to determine the reduction in road-user costs and indicates when resurfacing work is needed. New pavement roughness ratings—as measured by the international roughness index (IRI)—should range from 1.5 to 3.5; the higher the IRI, the rougher the pavement, with a roughness of 0 being perfectly smooth.

- *Average annual daily traffic*: A measure of the volume and type of traffic using a road.

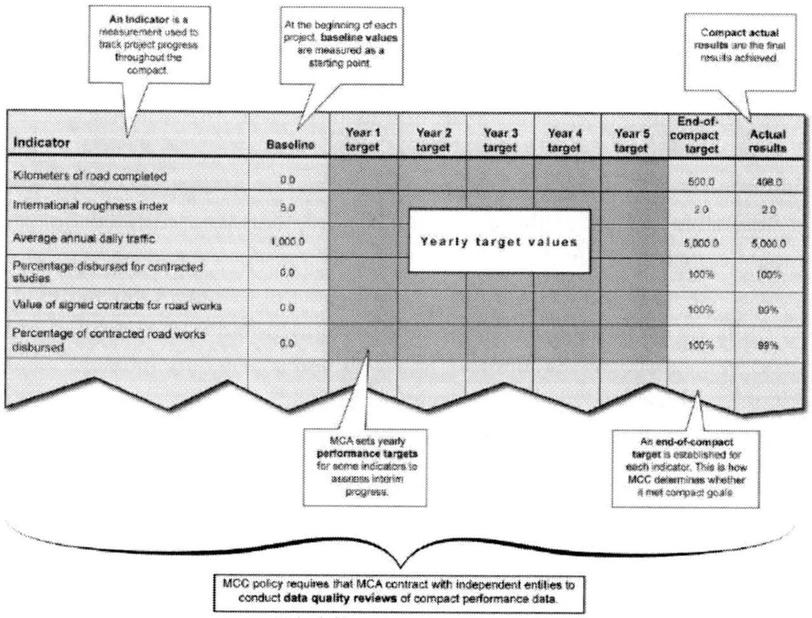

Source: GAO analysis.

Notes: The indicators shown are for a road project. The terms *indicator*, *baseline values*, *actual results*, *performance targets*, *end-of-compact target*, and *data quality reviews* pertain to all MCC projects.

Figure 2. Relationship between MCC Indicators, Baselines, Targets, and Results.

MCC has not established common indicators for ports, because ports are a small part of its portfolio (it has funded port projects in only two countries). However, we selected certain key indicators to review because they addressed the projects' key objective of economic growth:[13]

- *Volume of merchandise through the port:* A measure of the total volume of exports and imports passing through the port each year.
- *Container ship time at berth:* A measure of the average number of days a container ship spends at berth to load and/or unload its cargo.
- *Container ship time at anchor:* A measure of the average number of hours a container ship spends at anchor waiting for a berth.

Independent Data Quality Reviews

MCC requires that MCAs contract an independent entity (such as a local or international firm, research organization, or individual consultant) to review the quality of compact performance data. These reviews determine the utility, objectivity, and integrity of information gathered, identify problems with data quality, and recommend actions to remedy these issues. Reviews should ensure that data used to measure indicators meet the following criteria: validity, reliability, timeliness, precision, and integrity. MCC policy allows each country to determine the frequency and timing of each review as well as the indicators to be evaluated. This requirement was fulfilled for every compact except Nicaragua.

MCC policy requires the MCA to comment on the review, including noting the recommendations it will implement. In addition, the MCA should reflect, in a subsequent monitoring and evaluation plan, any indicator changes made in response to data quality reviews. MCC policy also requires the MCA to make publically available on its website a summary of the final reviews and its comments. MCAs are responsible for ensuring that MCC-approved recommendations are implemented.

Beneficiary Assessment

MCC defines beneficiaries as people who realize income gains or expenditure savings as a result of its investment.[14] MCC's authorizing legislation requires that compacts contain an identification of the intended beneficiaries, disaggregated by income level, gender, and age, to the maximum extent practicable. MCC notes that "the use of these [beneficiary] analyses and their availability to the general public are trademarks of MCC's commitment to transparency and results-based aid."

In addition, MCC's 2009 *Guidelines for Economic and Beneficiary Analysis* maintain that identification of intended beneficiaries should not be limited to counting the number of people who benefit from compacts but should include a more detailed analysis of the effect of compacts on different subgroups, including the poor, the elderly, women, children, and ethnic subpopulations. MCC has not undertaken such detailed beneficiary analysis for the seven compacts completed in 2010 or 2011.[15]

MCC Data Show That Some Key Performance Targets Were Met, but Data Quality Problems Call into Question Reported Results

MCC reduced the scope of early road and port projects and reports mixed success in meeting key performance targets. In addition, problems with data quality call those reported results into question.

MCC Reduced Targets for Completed Roads by 63 Percent and Had Data Quality Problems

In each of the six compacts with road projects, MCC reduced the number of kilometers to be completed. In addition, the roughness and annual average daily traffic indicators had data quality problems. Most compacts did not examine the three common road indicators in their data quality reviews. In addition, MCC did not consistently account for third-party funding.

According to MCC Data, Most Compacts Met Reduced Targets for Kilometers of Roads Completed

MCC reduced by 63 percent the total number of road kilometers to be completed for the six compacts with road projects, from an original combined target of 1,822.8 kilometers to a final combined target of 623.9 kilometers.[16] Five of six compacts met their reduced targets for kilometers completed. Honduras was the only compact that did not meet its target (see table 1).

In general, MCC decreased the scope of the road projects because of increased construction costs, changes in exchange rates, or actions taken by host country governments that were inconsistent with MCC's eligibility criteria. For example, MCC decreased the scope of the compacts in Nicaragua and Armenia because of concerns about democratic governance in the respective partner governments (see table 2).

MCC-Reported Results for Road Roughness Have Data Quality Issues

MCC data show that five of six compacts met original targets for road roughness. In addition, MCC reports that the Georgia and Armenia compacts surpassed their original roughness targets and built a smoother road than originally planned.[17] Honduras did not did not meet its roughness target. (See table 3.)

Table 1. Key Performance Results for the Kilometers of Road Completed Indicator, MCC Compacts Ending in 2010 and 2011

Country	Original target	Revised target	Percentage change	Final result	Target met
Honduras[a]	200.0	174.5	-12.8	115.0	x
Cape Verde	63.0	39.3	-37.6	40.6	○
Nicaragua	158.0	67.0	-57.6	74.0	○
Georgia	245.0	220.2	-10.1	220.2[b]	○
Vanuatu	213.8	149.7	-30.0	149.7	○
Armenia	943.0	24.4	-97.4	24.4	○
Total	1,822.8	675.1	-63.0	623.9	

Legend:

• Met original target.

○ Met revised target.

x Did not meet original or revised target.

Source: GAO analysis of MCC data.

Note: See appendix III for additional details on targets and results for the kilometers of road indicator in each country.

[a] Kilometers include secondary roads and sections 3 and 4 of the highway in Honduras. Sections 1 and 2 of the highway were to be completed post-compact with additional funding provided by the Central American Bank for Economic Integration; as of March 9, 2012, construction of these segments was not complete.

[b] Of this amount, 217 kilometers were fully rehabilitated using MCC funds. For the remaining about 3 kilometers, MCC funded maintenance items, such as road painting.

Table 2. Scope Revisions of Road Projects for MCC Compacts Ending in 2010 and 2011

Compact	Scope change	Reason for scope change
Honduras	Reduced kilometers of secondary roads completed. Removed two sections of the highway project, to be completed with additional funding from the Central American Bank for Economic Integration post-compact.	Increased construction costs.
Cape Verde	Eliminated two roads.	Increased construction costs.
Nicaragua	In June 2009, MCC terminated funding for the transportation activities not already under contract. At this time, 74 kilometers of road were already under construction.	Electoral irregularities in the municipal elections of November 2008, which were inconsistent with MCC eligibility criteria.a

Compact	Scope change	Reason for scope change
Georgia	Reduced kilometers of road to 70 percent of the original plan.	Increased construction costs and changes in exchange rates.
	Subsequently increased kilometers of road to roughly 90 percent of the original plan.	MCC obligated an additional $100 million to the compact following the end of Georgia's war with Russia over SouthOssetia in 2008, $60 million of which went to the road project.
Vanuatu	Reduced scope from the rehabilitation of several roads, airstrips and wharfs to two roads.	Increased construction costs and changes in exchange rates.
	Increased kilometers completed on road in Santo.	New Zealand provided additional funding to support MCC road project in June 2009.
Armenia	Reduced kilometers of road to roughly 32 percent of the original plan prior to June 2008.	Increased construction costs and changes in exchange rates.
	In June 2009, MCC put an indefinite hold on funding for road construction that was not already underway. At this time, construction of 24.4 kilometers had been completed.	Concerns about the status of democratic governance in Armenia, which were inconsistent with MCC's eligibility criteria.a

Source: GAO analysis of MCC documents.

[a] The country also failed to meet MCC's corruption indicator, which measures the extent to which public power is exercised for private gain.

Table 3. Key Performance Results for the Road Roughness Indicator, Compacts Ending in 2010 and 2011

Country	Original target	Revised target	Final result	Target met
Honduras[a]	2.2		3.0	x
Cape Verde	2.3		2.3	•
Nicaragua	3.1		2.5	•
Georgia	3.2	2.5	1.5	o
Vanuatu	3.5		3.0	•
Armenia	5.0	4.0	3.5	o

Legend:
- • Met original target.
- o Met revised target.
- x Did not meet original or revised target.

Source: GAO analysis of MCC data.

Notes: A higher roughness number indicates a rougher road, while zero is a perfectly smooth road. A missing value for the revised target indicates that the original target was not revised. See appendix III for additional details on targets and results for the roughness indicator in each country.

[a]The roughness measure includes secondary roads and sections 3 and 4 of the highway in Honduras. Sections 1 and 2 of the highway were to be completed post-compact with additional funding provided by the Central American Bank for Economic Integration; as of March 9, 2012, construction of these segments was not complete.

We identified problems with the measurement of road roughness for some of the six compacts with road projects, including the use of inconsistent application of methodologies and calculation errors. These problems call into question MCC's reported roughness results.

Inconsistent Application of Methodologies

MCC determined roughness using a visual scale for some roads and mechanical measurements for others. While both methods are legitimate means of measuring roughness, they have different degrees of accuracy. Moreover, MCC did not apply either measurement method consistently across compacts. First, for the two countries measuring roughness visually, Cape Verde and Vanuatu, MCC inappropriately provided the MCAs a World Bank scale for unpaved roads to assess the paved roads. Second, for compacts where roughness was measured mechanically, the MCAs used different machines that had varying levels of accuracy. Third, for three compacts—Nicaragua, Honduras, and Armenia—the MCAs measured roughness on both sides of the road and then averaged these measurements to calculate a final measure. In contrast, MCA-Georgia calculated roughness using measurements taken on one side of the road only, potentially producing a less accurate measurement since roughness can vary from one side of the road to the other.[18]

Calculation Errors

We found that errors calculating roughness led to an overstatement of results. For example, MCA-Nicaragua recorded zeros— an IRI rating for a perfectly smooth road—for sections that could not be measured, incorrectly lowering the overall roughness calculation from 4.8 to 3.4 for one road and indicating that the road was smoother than it actually was.[19] Additionally, MCA-Honduras did not account for the differing lengths of each segment of secondary road when aggregating the roughness values and therefore overstated its reported results at 3.2 instead of 3.3. Although this difference is not large, consistent methodologies should be used across compacts to allow a valid basis for comparing and evaluating results.

MCC-Reported Results for Road Traffic Have Data Quality Issues

MCC data show that three of the six compacts with road projects met original or revised targets for average annual daily traffic.[20] The Nicaragua and Armenia compacts met their original targets and the Vanuatu compact met a reduced target.

For the other three compacts, Cape Verde did not meet its original target; Georgia did not meet its reduced target; and MCC stated that a final traffic measure in Honduras is not expected until late 2012. (See table 4.)

Table 4. Key Performance Results for the Average Annual Daily Traffic Indicator, Compacts Ending in 2010 and 2011

Country	Original target	Revised target	Final result	Target met
Honduras[a]	3,772		N/A	N/A
Cape Verde[b]	559		295	x
Nicaragua	932		1,216	•
Georgia	6,700	1,183	1,092	x
Vanuatu	969	196	334	o
Armenia	460	706	735	o

Legend:

• Met original target.

o Met revised target.

X Did not meet original or revised target.

N/A Not available.

Source: GAO analysis of MCC data.

Notes: A missing value for the revised target indicates that the original target was not revised. See appendix III for additional details on targets and results for the traffic indicator in each country.

[a] The calculation for original and revised average annual daily traffic measures include the secondary roads and sections 3 and 4 of the highway in Honduras. Sections 1 and 2 of the highway were to be completed post-compact with additional funding provided by the Central American Bank for Economic Integration; as of March 9, 2012, construction of these segments was not complete. In addition, MCC officials stated that a final traffic measure in Honduras is not expected until late 2012.

[b] The final result for Cape Verde is not annualized.

MCC did not consistently update the baseline estimates for the annual average daily traffic indicator either by projecting growth or by using new information when it became available.

Because MCC establishes the targets for some indicators by applying estimated growth rates to the baselines, these identified weaknesses may have affected MCC's ability to create accurate traffic targets, thus affecting its reported results.

- For the secondary roads project in Nicaragua, MCC stated that it updated the baseline estimates established in 2007 by applying 1 year's growth rate to the traffic measures, because construction was expected to begin in fall 2008. However, MCC did not use this method in Cape Verde, where there was a similar time lag.[21]

- For the section of highway to be rehabilitated in Nicaragua, MCC retained a baseline calculated in a 2000 traffic study[22] even though it had 2007 data for the specific 18 kilometers of road it planned to rehabilitate.
- In Honduras, MCC used a baseline established before 2005 despite the availability of data from a 2008 traffic survey. The 2008 traffic survey results showed that traffic volumes already met or exceeded the end-of-compact targets for most road segments. Because MCC used the 2005 data, the final results for the project indicate a larger change over the compact implementation timeframe than actually occurred.

Common Indicators for Road Projects Not Consistently Reviewed for Quality

The data quality reviews conducted for most compacts did not include the kilometers-paved, roughness, or average annual daily traffic indicators. MCC requires that MCAs contract an independent entity to review the quality of compact performance data.

According to MCC, this requirement was fulfilled for every compact except Nicaragua. However, only the data quality reviews for Georgia included all three indicators. (The reviews did not identify any data problems with these indicators).[23]

Although the data quality reviews for Armenia included two of the three indicators, the compact was put on hold before MCA-Armenia could fully correct identified problems. In Vanuatu, data quality reviews conducted in 2008 and 2009 identified problems with the measurement of annual average daily traffic.[24] MCA-Vanuatu did not provide a response to either of the recommendations in the review and made no changes to the definition of the traffic indicator in the final monitoring and evaluation plan.

The data quality reviews for the Honduras and Cape Verde compacts did not include any of the three road indicators. Table 5 summarizes the treatment of the three common road indicators we examined in data quality reviews for the six compacts.

Table 5. Data Quality Reviews Performed for Road Project Common Indicators

Country	Kilometers of road completed	International roughness index	Average annual daily traffic	Recommendations implemented
Honduras	○	○	○	N/A
Cape Verde	○	○	○	N/A
Nicaragua[a]	X	X	X	N/A
Georgia	e	e	e	N/A
Vanuatu	○	○	●	No
Armenia	○	●	●	No[b]

Legend:
○ Indicator not reviewed.
◓ Indicator reviewed without recommendation.
● Indicator reviewed with recommendation.
X No data quality review performed.
N/A Not applicable.
Source: GAO analysis of MCA data quality reviews.
[a] MCC officials stated that no data quality reviews were performed in Nicaragua.
[b] Recommendations were not implemented in Armenia, because the road project was put on hold in June 2009.

MCC Did Not Consistently Account for Third-Party Funding

The governments of three countries—Honduras, Cape Verde, and Vanuatu—secured funding from a third party to rehabilitate some of the road lengths that MCC removed from the scope of the compact.[25] However, we found that MCC did not consistently account for this third-party funding when reporting the final results of kilometers completed. As a result, MCC understated its results in Honduras and overstated them in Vanuatu.

- The government of Honduras secured money from the Central American Bank for Economic Integration to complete 57.6 kilometers of the highway project, which MCC removed from the compact's original scope. [26] However, MCA-Honduras did not revise its kilometers-completed target to reflect this reduction in scope. Therefore, MCC reports that it did not meet the compact's final kilometers-completed target, even though data suggest that the kilometers MCC funded were complete at the end of the compact

- The government of Cape Verde secured funding from the government of Portugal to rehabilitate 22.9 kilometers of secondary roads that MCC removed from the scope of its compact. MCA-Cape Verde revised its kilometers-completed target to reflect this reduction in scope and did not report these 22.9 kilometers as a part of its final results. Therefore, MCC reports that it met the compact's revised kilometers-completed target.
- The government of Vanuatu secured money from New Zealand to assist in rehabilitating a 57.2 kilometer road, because the MCC compact funds were not sufficient to complete all 57.2 kilometers. However, MCC reported all 57.2 kilometers as a part of its final results, even though it did not fund all of the work.

MCC Reduced the Cape Verde Port Project Scope and Did Not Meet Many Targets for the Benin Port Project

For the Cape Verde compact, MCC reduced the scope of the port project, deferred the measurement of key indicators, and therefore did not conduct any data quality reviews of those indicators. In Benin, MCC completed most of the originally envisioned port project scope, and its data show that the compact met the original target for one of the three key indicators. However, we identified issues with the indicators' baseline estimates. In addition, data quality reviews identified problems with the data behind the indicators, which MCA-Benin did not formally address.

In Cape Verde, MCC Reduced the Port Project's Scope and Deferred the Measurement of Key Indicators

MCC split the Cape Verde project into two phases in May 2008 because, owing to increased construction costs, the $53.7 million allocated to the port projects was insufficient to fund all of the planned improvements. MCC funded phase 1 of the improvements, including construction of a cargo storage area and an access road, and rehabilitation of Wharf 2. The government of Cape Verde secured a loan from the government of Portugal for $87 million to complete phase 2, that is, those elements removed from the scope of the MCC project.[27] The MCC-funded portion of the construction (phase 1) represents about one-third of the total expected cost of both phases. Nearly 100 percent of the works for phase 1 were completed by compact end. Phase 2 was awarded late in the compact, and work was under way as of July 2012.

MCC deferred the measurement of key performance indicators when it revised the project scope, because results for key indicators could be measured only after full completion of the port (see table 6). MCC intends to measure results for the key indicators when phase 2 is complete.

Table 6. Key Performance Results for MCC Port Project in Cape Verde

Indicator	Original target	Revised target	Final result	Targetmet
Volume of merchandise (thousand tons/year)	710.5	Performance indicators were eliminated once the Cape Verde project was descoped.		
Container ship time at berth (days)	1.0			
Container ship time at anchor (hours)	4.0			

Source: GAO analysis of MCC data.

Note: See appendix IV for additional details on targets and results for key indicators in Cape Verde.

MCA-Cape Verde contracted for data quality reviews in 2007 and 2010. The port project was reviewed in 2010; however, key indicators were not evaluated, because MCA-Cape Verde deferred measurement of those indicators until phase 2 was complete.

MCC's Reported Results for the Benin Port Project Have Data Quality Issues

MCC data show that Benin maintained most of the original project scope and met the original target for one of three key indicators.[28] The project scope included constructing or rehabilitating a jetty, a new wharf, and port roads and installing lighting, security, and an electricity distribution system. MCC reports that the Benin compact met the original target for volume of merchandise through the port, but it did not meet targets for the other two key indicators, container ship waiting time at berth and container ship waiting time at anchor. See table 7 for a summary of key performance results for the Benin port project.

We identified problems with MCC's measurement of the volume-of-merchandise indicators, and MCA-Benin's data quality reviews identified additional problems with all three key indicators. For the volume-of-merchandise indicator in Benin, MCC used 2004 data from the Port Authority to establish a baseline of 4.1 million metric tons in the compact's monitoring and evaluation plans and indicator tracking tables. MCA-Benin did not subsequently update the baseline. However, the compact did not enter into force until October 2006 and port improvement construction did not begin until August 2009. Available annual data for Benin showed that in 2005 the volume of merchandise had already increased to 5.2 million metric tons. Without an updated baseline, the estimate may not accurately reflect preconstruction conditions and may lead MCC to overstate the degree to which port traffic increased because of the compact.

Table 7. Key Performance Results for MCC Port Project in Benin

Indicator	Original target	Revised target	Final result	Targetmet
Volume of merchandise (thousand tons/year)	6,944.6		7,605.9	●
Container ship time at berth (days)	1.0		1.3	x
Container ship time at anchor (hours)	4.0		34.6	x

Legend:

● Met original target.

o Met revised target.

x Did not meet original or revised target.

Source: GAO analysis of MCC data.

Note: A missing value for the revised target indicates that the original target was not revised. See appendix IV for additional details on targets and results for key indicators in Benin.

MCA-Benin contracted data quality reviews in 2008, 2009, and 2011. The 2008 and 2009 data quality reviews identified issues with the three key port indicators that we reviewed, but MCC did not address all of the issues.[29] The 2011 review did not examine these specific port indicators.

- For the volume-of-merchandise indicator, MCA-contractors noted that although data collection methods were consistent and the data were valid, the Port Authority of Cotonou needed to improve the timeliness of data related to this indicator because the data entry and control procedures created delays in the availability of information. MCC policy indicates that data should be sufficiently current to inform management decisions because decisions depend on regular collection of performance information. In 2008 and 2009, the contractors recommended that MCA-Benin set up an automatic data transfer system for information collected on ship stopover, to avoid redundant data entry efforts by the port's statistical services. Although the 2009 review indicated that the port was resolving problems through the creation of a port information system when the evaluation was conducted, we found that MCA-Benin did not resolve the issues identified for this indicator. No changes were made in the final monitoring and evaluation plan to indicate that adjustments were made in the data collection methods for this indicator. In addition, MCA-Benin responses to the review did not address this issue.

- For the container ship time at berth and container ship time at anchor indicators, the 2008 and 2009 reviews noted that, while the data collected were a direct measure of what the indicators were intended to capture and the data collection procedures were consistent, there were no historical data to support the baseline values for these indicators. The reviews recommended using baseline values established in a 2005 report by an international consulting firm. We found that MCA-Benin did not resolve issues identified for these two indicators. MCC and MCA officials stated that they decided not to revise indicator baselines and targets as recommended, and no revisions were made to baseline figures in subsequent monitoring and evaluation plans. MCC and MCA officials provided no additional explanation.

DATA RESULTING FROM BENEFICIARY CALCULATIONS MAY NOT BE VALID

In 2009, MCC improved its beneficiary estimates by adopting a more standardized approach, which it documented in its *Guidelines for Economic and Beneficiary Analysis;* however, the updated guidelines do not include a formal quality review process. MCC subsequently revised its beneficiary estimates for ongoing compacts, but the implementation of the new approach was not always consistent and suffered from varying degrees of quality control problems.

Although some of the individual problems we identified were small in nature, taken as a whole they reduce confidence in MCC's estimates.

MCC's Updated Beneficiary Analysis Guidelines Do Not Include a Formal Quality Review Process

In our previous work, we found that MCC did not have a consistent methodology for estimating the number of beneficiaries across compacts.[30] As a result, MCC adopted a new, more standardized approach, which it published in its 2009 *Guidelines for Economic and Beneficiary Analysis*. MCC subsequently conducted a "beneficiary scrub," revising beneficiary numbers for ongoing compacts based on the 2009 guidelines. However, we found errors and inconsistencies in the calculations. MCC stated that these scrubs are informally reviewed but that they do not undergo a formal quality review process.[31] Such a process would ensure that the information and data provided have been verified for consistency and accuracy.

Weaknesses Call into Question the Validity and Reliability of MCC's Beneficiary Data

We identified three general weaknesses with MCC's beneficiary calculations. First, the beneficiary calculations in MCC's internal documents contain weaknesses such as incorrect formulas and numbers as well as discrepancies with supporting documents. Second, MCC did not apply a consistent methodology in estimating beneficiaries for its early transportation infrastructure projects. Third, the beneficiary figures in MCC's public documents are sometimes inaccurate.

MCC's Beneficiary Calculations Contained Mistakes

Some beneficiary calculations contained mistakes in the formulas used. For example, the computations of the population growth rate for Georgia and Cape Verde contained an error in the mathematical formula, causing MCC to slightly overstate the growth rate in the first case and understate it in the second case. In addition, erroneous numbers were used in four of the seven compacts we reviewed.

- For the Georgia road project, MCC stated in the beneficiary calculation documents that "the original beneficiary estimate of 53,988 people counts all households living in the four rayons, or districts, through which the road passes...The revised beneficiary estimate [of 58,079] is based on a 5 km catchment area of the Road."

MCC thus originally claimed a lower number of beneficiaries for a larger geographic area (the districts) than the more limited catchment area— the geographic area in which benefits may be expected to accrue—of 5 kilometers on either side of the road.[32]

- For the Benin port project, the population projection in the beneficiary scrub began with a 2005 original baseline figure of 8,490,000, since the port project is expected to raise the incomes of the entire population of Benin. However, this number could not be derived from its purported source, the 2002 population census.[33]
- For the Armenia road project, the document supporting the beneficiary scrub calculation considered a catchment area for an erroneous revised road length of 68 kilometers rather than the correct figure of 24.4 kilometers.
- In the Cape Verde roads and bridges activity, the original beneficiary numbers provided in the document supporting the beneficiary scrub spreadsheet did not match the figures in the spreadsheet.

MCC's Methodology to Estimate Beneficiaries Is Not Consistently Applied across Compacts

In the 2009 revision of its *Guidelines for Economic and Beneficiary Analysis,* MCC standardized its methodology to estimate beneficiaries and accordingly modified its beneficiary numbers in the spreadsheets for its beneficiary scrubs. However, the amount of detail in the analysis varied across compacts, and population growth rates were not always calculated in a consistent manner.

Of the beneficiary scrubs we reviewed, four of seven contained disaggregated data at the project level. Specifically, the Armenia, Georgia, Nicaragua, and Vanuatu scrubs are made up of multiple, relatively detailed spreadsheets. By contrast, one beneficiary scrub, for Honduras, contained one page of macro-level summary data with no explanation or sources for the figures. The remaining two of the seven scrubs contained additional data but were not as detailed as the first four. For example, the Cape Verde scrub included a second sheet of World Bank development indicators on the country, and the Benin scrub had some details on one of the compact projects. These varying levels of detail suggest that the scrubs were executed in an ad hoc, rather than consistent, manner.

MCC uses population growth rates to estimate the number of beneficiaries in a 20-year projection period; for each compact, MCC publicly presents the number of beneficiaries projected for the end of the 20-year period.[34]

However, the scrub sheets we reviewed showed that MCC sometimes computed population growth rates differently across compacts, even when the scrubs provided the same underlying information.

- For Honduras, MCC indicated that it took the population growth rates for 2005, 2006, and 2007 from World Bank data and averaged the three rates to get an average annual growth rate for the projection.[35]
- For Georgia and Cape Verde, MCC did not use the historical growth rates provided but instead took total population figures in 2005 and 2007 and used them to compute an average annual growth rate for the beneficiary projection.
- For Vanuatu, MCC computed an average annual growth rate based on four historical growth rates without specifying a source or year.

For Some Countries, MCC Did Not Update Beneficiary Numbers or Reported Them Incorrectly

In three of seven compacts, we found that some numbers in MCC's public documents had not been updated or were inaccurate.

- In the case of the Georgia road, a December 2009 report and a July 2011 close-out document used original beneficiary estimates (53,988), instead of using the revised estimate (58,079) from July 2009, when MCC reported having recalculated the beneficiary numbers. In addition, in the 2011 status report, the total number of beneficiaries for the compact as a whole (143,000) was smaller than the beneficiaries of the infrastructure project alone (300,000).
- For the Benin port project, the beneficiary estimate that appeared in a 2011 status report (8,791,832) was an original estimate from 2009 instead of the revised estimate of 16,119,058. In addition, the supporting document accompanying the 2009 scrub spreadsheet mistakenly reported 13,421,086 beneficiaries for the port project by 2026. However, the data in the scrub indicated that this figure referred to the number of beneficiaries in 2020; the correct number of projected beneficiaries for 2026 is 16,119,058.
- For Armenia, the beneficiary estimate for the road project in a 2011 publication (6,216) did not reflect a revision of the estimate done in 2009 (6,356).

CONCLUSION

MCC recognizes the importance of a disciplined, transparent, and accountable approach to tracking compact results to make well-informed decisions about U.S. investments. It has established an extensive monitoring and evaluation program that includes guidance and tools for the partner countries and controls on data quality. In addition, MCC has created and implemented a revised beneficiary calculation methodology to ensure standardization across projects and compacts.

Even with these steps, problems exist with the data behind several of MCC's key performance indicators, limiting the reliability of MCC's reported results.

- MCAs have not measured the results of common indicators in a uniform manner—including how they account for additional third-party funding—nor have they consistently reviewed the quality of data used to report the indicators' results. As such, MCC cannot confidently compare or aggregate the results of these common indicators as intended.
- MCC requires the establishment of baselines to measure the impact its assistance has on partner countries. However, because some incorrect baselines were used, results may be over- or understated.
- MCAs have not consistently fulfilled the MCC requirements that they conduct independent data quality reviews and respond to issues the reviews raised. As a result, MCC and its partners have missed opportunities to improve data quality and facilitate data reporting and aggregation.

In addition, MCC's beneficiary calculations have problems that limit their usefulness. Because MCC's new approach to estimating beneficiary numbers does not include a formal quality review process, the beneficiary estimates contain incorrect numbers and formulas and inconsistent calculations. While the impact of these problems is generally small, the lack of a robust, formal quality review process nonetheless calls into question the reliability of MCC's estimates. Without a correct representation of the compacts' results and beneficiaries, MCC, Congress, and other key stakeholders cannot accurately evaluate the extent to which MCC is achieving its goals of poverty reduction and economic growth.

RECOMMENDATIONS FOR EXECUTIVE ACTION

We recommend that MCC's Chief Executive Officer take the following four actions.

To improve the reliability of results measurement, MCC should

- improve guidance for common indicators by requiring that they are included in data quality reviews, measured uniformly across compacts, and reported in a standardized manner—including when third-party funding is used to complete the original scope of a project;
- improve guidance for baseline measurements by requiring MCAs to document the date, source, and methodology for establishing the baseline; and
- enforce current monitoring and evaluation policy requiring MCAs to conduct data quality reviews and to provide written comments in response to identified issues, discussing how recommendations will be implemented or explaining why changes may not be made.

To ensure more accurate beneficiary numbers, MCC should

- incorporate into the *Guidelines for Economic and Beneficiary Analysis* a formal process for reviewing beneficiary calculations and analysis.

AGENCY COMMENTS AND OUR EVALUATION

In written comments on a draft of this report, MCC stated that it agrees with our four recommendations and outlined steps it will take or has taken to address them.

- With respect to our first recommendation—to improve guidance for common indicators—MCC stated that it has taken preliminary actions to address it. We reviewed MCC's May 2012 *Guidance on Common Indicators* and found that it defines the indicators and specifies each indicator's unit of measurement and how each should be disaggregated. In addition, when MCC activities are conducted jointly with other organizations (e.g. when the activities include third-party funding), MCC's guidance instructs MCAs to report only MCC's contribution to a particular common indicator. In addition, the guidance states that MCC will be explicit in reporting which changes in outcome indicators are more likely the result of MCC investments and which changes might also be influenced by other interventions. However, the guidance lacks enough specificity to address other weaknesses we identified. For example, when discussing road roughness, the guidance does not instruct MCAs to measure both sides of the road to account for variation in roughness from one side of the road to the other. In addition, this guidance does not specify that MCAs should include common indicators in their data quality reviews.

- With respect to our second recommendation—to improve guidance for baseline measurements—MCC stated that its current monitoring and evaluation policy requires that compacts' monitoring and evaluation plans document the date, source, and methodology for establishing baseline measurements. MCC further stated that current MCA monitoring and evaluation plans are compliant with this requirement.
- With respect to our third recommendation—to enforce current monitoring and evaluation policy requiring MCAs to conduct data quality reviews and to provide written comments in response to identified issues—MCC stated that it works with MCAs to ensure that recommendations of data quality reviews are incorporated into monitoring and evaluation plans and then implemented.
- With respect to our fourth recommendation—to incorporate a formal process for reviewing beneficiary calculations and analysis—MCC noted that it will institute a formal process for reviewing beneficiary calculations and address the weaknesses we identified in this report.

MCC asserted that the results of its compact investments are not diminished by the data quality challenges highlighted in this report. MCC noted, for example, that more than 623 kilometers of rehabilitated roads now serve poor and rural households in the countries we reviewed, linking farmers to markets and bolstering important regional trade routes. Regarding our finding that the total target for kilometers of road completed for the six compacts was reduced by 63 percent, MCC also noted that the final target for Honduras, Georgia, Cape Verde, and Vanuatu would be only 19 percent below the original target if we were to exclude the road projects that MCC terminated or discontinued as a result of the Armenian and Nicaraguan governments' undemocratic behavior.

We incorporated technical comments from MCC in our report where appropriate.

David Gootnick
Director
International Affairs and Trade

APPENDIX I: OBJECTIVES, SCOPE, AND METHODOLOGY

The fiscal year 2008 Consolidated Appropriations Act, Public Law 110 161, mandated that GAO review the results of the Millennium Challenge Corporation's (MCC) compacts. This report examines the extent to which MCC has, for transportation infrastructure projects in compacts ending in 2010 and 2011, (1) achieved expected performance targets and (2) used a consistent methodology in estimating numbers of beneficiaries. The seven countries with compacts relevant to our scope are Honduras, Cape Verde, Nicaragua, Georgia, Vanuatu, Armenia, and Benin.

MCC enters into a legal relationship with partner country governments, which vests responsibility for day-to-day management of compact project implementation with an accountable entity—a Millennium Challenge Account (MCA)—including monitoring and evaluation activities such as setting and revising targets. Because such MCA actions require MCC's direct oversight and approval, throughout this report we attribute all decisions related to project rescoping and compact targets to MCC.

To assess the extent to which MCC has achieved its performance targets for transportation infrastructure projects in compacts ending in 2010 and 2011, we reviewed MCC guidance and policy documents and analyzed compacts, monitoring and evaluation plans, and indicator tracking tables for the compacts with Honduras, Cape Verde, Nicaragua, Georgia, Vanuatu, Armenia, and Benin. In assessing and reporting MCC's results, we compared actual results achieved at the end of the compact for select performance indicators with the original and, in some cases, revised targets associated with each indicator. We considered the original target to be the one first documented for each performance indicator and the final target to be the one last documented in MCC monitoring documents.

Given that MCC tracks several performance indicators for each compact project, we selected a subset of indicators to examine for this report. For the roads projects, we examined kilometers of road completed, road roughness, and average annual daily traffic. We selected these road project indicators because (1) they address the projects' key objectives and (2) they are among the "common indicators" that MCC requires all road projects to measure so that it can aggregate results across countries. For the port projects, we examined volume of merchandise through the port, container ship time at berth, and container ship time at anchor. Although MCC has not established common indicators for the port projects, we selected these port project indicators because they (1) addressed the projects' key objectives, (2) corresponded to the common indicators established for the roads projects, and (3) were originally included in both port projects.

To report the average value of targets and results for compact road projects, we calculated a weighted average using the length of each road segment. We performed this calculation for the average annual daily traffic and roughness indicators for Cape Verde, Honduras, Vanuatu, and Nicaragua because these MCAs report targets and results by road segment. For Honduras, we did not weight the indicators using values from sections 1 and 2 because the government of Honduras completed these sections with funding from the Central American Bank for Economic Integration. For Cape Verde, we did not include the average annual daily traffic and roughness for bridge projects, because the kilometer lengths of these sections were not available.

To determine the amount of funding used for transportation infrastructure projects, we reviewed MCC financial data. We included compact implementation funding—funds disbursed before entry into force to facilitate the implementation of the compact—with other projects not related to transportation infrastructure.

To determine which MCAs contracted for independent data quality reviews, which transportation infrastructure indicators were evaluated, and whether recommendations were made for common and key indicators, we reviewed third-party data quality review reports. To determine whether recommendations were implemented, we reviewed MCA comments on the data quality reviews that MCC provided to us and we reviewed final monitoring and evaluation plans.

To assess the extent to which MCC has consistently applied its beneficiary estimation methodology, we reviewed MCC's beneficiary calculations and accompanying supporting documents for the seven compacts that ended in 2010 and 2011.

In particular, we examined for consistency and accuracy the data and formulas on projected beneficiaries for road and port projects in the Excel spreadsheets that MCC used to update—or "scrub"—the beneficiary estimates. We reviewed the documents explaining the calculations. We compared original beneficiary figures for these transportation projects with the revised ones and assessed the justification behind the changes.

We also examined quarterly status reports and the monitoring and evaluation plans for each compact to check the accuracy of the publicly reported beneficiary counts. We consulted with MCC officials when we found discrepancies and errors in the data.

As part of related GAO engagements focusing on Cape Verde and Honduras[1] and on Georgia and Benin,[2] we visited compact projects in-country and met with MCA officials, partner country government officials, contractors, project managers, construction supervisors, and relevant private businesses.

Data are considered reliable when they are accurate, complete, consistent and valid, given the uses for which they are intended.

To assess the reliability of MCC indicator and beneficiary data, we (1) reviewed MCC policy for the monitoring and evaluation of compacts and for calculating beneficiary numbers, (2) interviewed MCC and MCA officials regarding the reliability and validity of the data, (3) reviewed independent data quality reviews required by MCC, (4) compared performance indicators across original and final monitoring and evaluation plans and indicator tracking tables to identify inconsistencies, and (5) reviewed beneficiary calculations for accuracy. We identified some weaknesses in the data that may affect the data's reliability, as discussed in this report.

Finally, some of the reports and documents referenced above were written in French and Spanish. We translated these documents as needed, creating English summaries to enable our analysis.

We conducted this performance audit from August 2011 to September 2012 in accordance with generally accepted government auditing standards.[3] Those standards require that we plan and perform the audit to obtain sufficient, appropriate evidence to provide a reasonable basis for our findings and conclusions based on our audit objectives.

We believe the evidence obtained provides a reasonable basis for our findings and conclusions based on our audit objectives.

Appendix II: Compact Timeframes

The Millennium Challenge Corporation (MCC) completed seven compacts in 2010 and 2011—Honduras, Cape Verde, Nicaragua, Georgia, Benin, Vanuatu, and Armenia (see fig. 3). MCC commits funding when it signs a compact, but MCC does not obligate funding until the compact enters into force. MCC funding that the partner country does not spend for compact activities by the end of the 5-year implementation timeframe must be deobligated.[1]

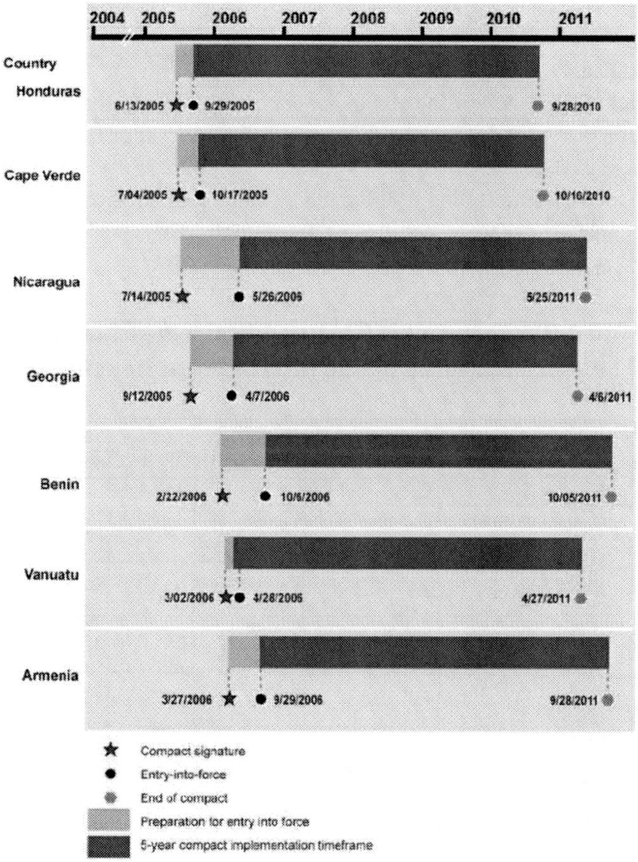

Source: GAO analysis of MCC compact data.

Figure 3. Timeframes for MCC Compacts Ending in 2010 and 2011, by Date of Signature.

APPENDIX III: ROADS DATA

Table 8. Kilometers of Roads Completed for MCC Road Projects in Compacts Ending in 2010 and 2011

Country	Original target	Final target	Final result	Percentage of original target met	Percentage of final target met
Honduras	200.0	174.5[a]	115.0	57.5	65.9
Cape Verde	63.0	39.3	40.6	64.4	103.3
Nicaragua	158.0	67.0	74.0	46.8	110.4
Georgia	245.0	220.2	220.0	89.8	100.0
Vanuatu	213.8	149.7	149.7	70.0	100.0
Armenia[b]	943.0	24.4	24.4	2.6	100.0

Source: GAO analysis of MCC data.

[a] After reducing the scope of the Honduras compact, MCC formally reduced the final target for the secondary road activities but did not reduce the final target for the highway activity.

[b] MCC provided documentation of kilometers completed; however, the documentation did not include takeover certificates from contractors, the data source for final kilometers in other countries.

Table 9. Road Roughness of MCC Road Projects in Compacts ending in 2010 and 2011, as Measured by the International Roughness Index (IRI)

Country	Road section	Roughness baseline	Original target	Final target	Final result	IRI methodology[a]
Honduras[b]						
	CA-5 Highway: Section 1	4.7	1.9	1.9	N/C	
	CA-5 Highway: Section 2	4.4	1.9	1.9	N/C	
	CA-5 Highway: Section 3	4.0	1.9	1.9	2.2	Mechanical
	CA-5 Highway: Section 4	4.0	1.9	1.9	3.2	Mechanical
	Secondary roads	13.6	2.5	2.5	3.2	Mechanical
Cape Verde						
	Road 1: Orgãos-Pedra Badejo	19.0	2.0	2.0	2.0	Visual
	Road 2: Cruz Grande-Calhetona	18.0	2.0	2.0	2.0	Visual
	Road 4: Assomada-Rincão	20.7	2.0	2.0	2.0	Visual
	Road: Vila das Pombas-Eito	18.0	10.0	10.0	10.0	Visual

Country	Road section	Roughness baseline	Original target	Final target	Final result	IRI methodology[a]
Nicaragua						
	Highway N-1: Villanueva-Guasaule	12.0	3.4	3.4	1.8	Mechanical
	S1: Somotillo-Cinco Pinos	13.2	3.0	3.0	3.4	Mechanical
	S9: Leon-Poneloya	12.0	3.0	3.0	1.8	Mechanical
Georgia		16.6	3.2	2.5	1.5	Mechanical
Vanuatu						
	Efate Ring Road	17.5	3.5	3.5	3.0	Visual
	Santo East Coast Road	22.0	3.5	3.5	3.0	Visual
Armenia	14.2	5.0	4.0	3.5	14.2	Mechanical

Source: GAO analysis of MCC data.

N/C = not complete.

Note: We found weaknesses in some of the reported data on road roughness, including the use of inconsistent application of methodologies and calculation errors.

[a] There are two standard methods for measuring IRI: mechanical reading and visual observation. Mechanical reading involves using a device such as a bump integrator, walking profiler, or car-mounted software equipment to measure the IRI for each kilometer of road, which is then averaged across the length of the road to provide a single IRI estimate. The margin of error for mechanical readings differs depending on the type of device used. Visual observation is based on interpreting the smoothness of an observers' drive of the road at different speeds in a standard passenger vehicle, as corresponding to an IRI visual assessment scale. The accuracy of the visual inspection varies with the experience of the observer.

[b] Because of the rescoping of the Honduras compact, sections 1 and 2 of the CA-5 Highway were completed post-compact with additional funding provided by the Central American Bank for Economic Integration; as of March 9, 2012, construction of these segments was not complete.

Table 10. Average Annual Daily Traffic on MCC-Funded Roads in Compacts Ending in 2010 and 2011

Country		Average annual daily traffic baseline	Original target	Final target	Final result
Honduras[a]					
	CA-5 Highway: Section 1	8,374	9,447	9,447	N/C
	CA-5 Highway: Section 2	5,411	6,104	6,104	N/C

Table 10. (Continued)

Country		Average annual daily traffic baseline	Original target	Final target	Final result
	CA-5 Highway: Sections 3 & 4	6,732	7,594	7,594	N/C
	Secondary roads	676	887	887	N/C
Cape Verde[b]					
	Road 1: Orgãos-Pedra Badejo	298	375	375	432
	Road 2: Cruz Grande-Calhetona	440	554	554	235
	Road 4: Assomada-Rincão	543	684	684	268
	Road: Vila das Pombas-Eito	410	517	517	184
	Bridge Ribeira Grande-Paul	552	695	695	76
	Bridge Ribeira da Torre-Ponta de Sol	765	963	963	644
	Bridge A Paul (Vila das Pombas)	671	845	845	50
	Highway N-1: Villanueva-Guasaule	1,413	1,580	1,580	1,962
	S1: Somotillo-Cinco Pinos	234	278	278	561
	S9: Leon-Poneloya	1,103	1,276	1,276	1,462
Georgia		612	6,700	1,183	1,092
Vanuatu					
	Efate Ring Road	85	950	98	305
	Santo East Coast Road	307	1,000	355	381
Armenia		637	460	706	735

Source: GAO analysis of MCC data.

N/C = not complete.

Note: We found weaknesses in some of the reported data on average annual daily traffic, including inconsistent updating of baseline measurements.

[a] A traffic count for completed roads in Honduras was conducted from December 19, 2010, through January 25, 2011. MCC stated that it does not expect a final traffic measure in Honduras until late 2012.

[b] As of January 2012, a final traffic study for completed roads in Cape Verde had not been conducted; results shown reflect traffic counts conducted at the compact end date and do not reflect annualized average daily traffic volumes.

APPENDIX IV: PORT DATA

Table 11. Volume of Merchandise through Port for Projects in MCC Compacts That Ended in 2010 and 2011

Thousand tons/year				
Country	Baseline	Original target	Final target	Final result
Cape Verde[a]	482	711	711	N/C
Benin	4,519[b]	6,945	6,945	7,606

Source: GAO analysis of MCC data.

N/C = not complete.

[a] MCC eliminated performance indicators after decreasing the scope of the Cape Verde port project, because the indicators could not be measured prior to completion of the Phase II works, including the wharf 1, container yard, and breakwater. Phase II was funded by the government of Portugal and was expected to be completed after the compact closed.

[b] Baseline from 2004. According to MCC, the value in 2005 was 5,680 thousand tons. If MCC had used 2005 data for its baseline, the volume of merchandise would not show as large an increase.

Table 12. Container Ship Time at Berth for Port Projects in MCC Compacts That Ended in 2010 and 2011

Days				
Country	Baseline	Original target	Final target	Final result
Cape Verde[a]	1.41	1.01	1.01	N/C
Benin	2	1	1	1.31

Source: GAO analysis of MCC data.

N/C = not complete

[a] MCC eliminated performance indicators after descoping the Cape Verde port project, because the indicators could not be measured prior to completion of the Phase II works, including the wharf 1, container yard, and breakwater. Phase II was funded by the government of Portugal and was expected to be completed after the compact closed.

Table 13. Container Ship Time at Anchor for Port Projects in MCC Compacts That Ended in 2010 and 2011

Hours				
Country	Baseline	Original target	Final target	Final result
Cape Verde[a]	5	4	4	N/C
Benin	16	4	4	34.6

Source: GAO analysis of MCC data.

N/C = not complete.

[a] MCC eliminated performance indicators after descoping the Cape Verde Port project, because the indicators could not be measured prior to completion of the Phase II works, including the wharf 1, container yard, and breakwater. Phase II was funded by the government of Portugal and was expected to be completed after the compact closed.

End Notes

[1] MCC commits funding when a compact is signed and obligates funds after the compact enters into force. As of June 2012, MCC had signed initial compacts with, in order of signature, Madagascar, Honduras, Cape Verde, Nicaragua, Georgia, Benin, Vanuatu, Armenia, Ghana, Mali, El Salvador, Mozambique, Lesotho, Morocco, Mongolia, Tanzania, Burkina Faso, Namibia, Senegal, Moldova, the Philippines, Jordan, Malawi, Indonesia, and Zambia. In February 2012, MCC signed a second compact with Cape Verde.

[2] We did not include the Madagascar compact in this review because, as the result of an undemocratic transfer of power in Madagascar in March 2009, MCC formally terminated the compact effective August 31, 2009, before the end of the 5-year statutory compact timeframe.

[3] *Consolidated Appropriations Act, 2008*, Pub. L. No. 110-161, § 668(d)(1)(A). The Act also required us to examine the financial control and procurement practices of MCC and its accountable entities. We responded to this requirement separately in GAO, *Millennium Challenge Corporation: MCC Has Addressed a Number of Implementation Challenges, but Needs to Improve Financial Controls and Infrastructure Planning*, GAO-10-52 (Washington, D.C.: Nov. 6, 2009).

[4] GAO, *Millennium Challenge Corporation: Compacts in Cape Verde and Honduras Achieved Reduced Targets,* GAO-11-728 (Washington, D.C.: Jul. 25, 2011).

[5] GAO, *Millennium Challenge Corporation: Georgia and Benin Transportation Infrastructure Projects Varied in Quality and May Not Be Sustainable,* GAO-12-630 (Washington, D.C.: Jun. 27, 2012).

[6] GAO-11-728 and GAO-12-630.

[7] Other board members are the U.S. Trade Representative, the Administrator of the U.S. Agency for International Development, the Chief Executive Officer of MCC, and up to four Senate-confirmed nongovernmental members appointed by the President from lists of individuals submitted by congressional leadership.

[8] MCC generally refers to each country's accountable entity by combining MCA with the country's name (e.g., MCA-Benin).

[9] MCC developed guidelines in 2006 to assist eligible countries in the preparation of monitoring and evaluation plans and issued an updated policy in 2009 and in 2012.

[10] In many cases, indicators are chosen because they relate to inputs for the economic rate of return analysis that MCC conducts to estimate a project's likely impact on the partner country's economic growth and poverty reduction prior to compact approval. More specifically, a project's estimated economic rate of return is the expected annual average return to the country's firms, individuals, or sectors for each dollar that MCC spends on the project.

[11] MCC issued its Common Indicators Directive in 2009, establishing the common indicators and requiring MCAs to use them in project monitoring and evaluation plans. Although the seven compacts that we reviewed were signed before 2009, initial monitoring and evaluation plans for three of the six compacts with road projects included common indicators for kilometers completed, road roughness, and average annual daily traffic. The MCAs for the three remaining compacts introduced the common indicators into their monitoring and evaluation activities before the compacts ended.

[12] MCC has developed additional common indicators for roads, including the percentage of funds disbursed for contracted studies, value of signed contracts for road works, percentage of funds for contracted road works disbursed, kilometers of roads under works contracts, and

value of signed contracts for feasibility design supervision and program management contracts.

[13] MCC has developed other indicators for ports, including percentage of funds for contracted port works disbursed, average time for goods to clear customs, average duration of stay of trucks at port, tons of merchandise shipped per year, and whether the port is meeting the International Ship and Port Facility Code, which establishes security requirements for ports.

[14] According to its *Guidelines for Economic and Beneficiary Analysis,* MCC takes the household as the unit of measurement, counting as beneficiaries all members of the household. MCC's projects include targeted projects that benefit specific individuals or households—for example, projects focused on agricultural development or school construction—but also includes projects that are national or broad-based in scope and benefit people living in a large geographical area. Beneficiaries include everyone who realizes income gain or expenditure savings regardless of the magnitude of these changes, although the income gain or expenditure savings are likely to vary significantly across individuals and projects.

[15] MCC officials stated that detailed beneficiary analyses for its compacts are carried out retrospectively. MCC provided us with detailed beneficiary analyses, including "poverty scorecards" focusing on the impact of compacts on the poor, for six other compacts out of the 26 current and completed compacts.

[16] In response to a draft copy of this report, MCC noted that if one excludes road projects that MCC terminated or discontinued as a result of undemocratic behavior by the governments of Armenia and Nicaragua, the final target for kilometers of roads completed in Honduras, Georgia, Cape Verde, and Vanuatu is only 19 percent below the original target. See appendix V for a copy of MCC's comments.

[17] In Georgia, MCC reduced the roughness target to account for a delayed construction start date. A road's surface is smoothest directly following construction. Because the delay in construction pushed the expected completion date closer to the compact end date, this reduced the amount of time MCC-funded roads could deteriorate before roughness measurements were taken at the end of the compact. Therefore, the roads were expected to have a better roughness measure than originally planned. In Armenia, MCC reduced the target for road roughness once the project was placed on indefinite hold. The 24.4 kilometers that MCC completed before putting the project on hold had a lower roughness target than the full package of roads MCC originally planned to complete. Therefore, removing the terminated roads from the project resulted in a better roughness measure for the compact overall.

[18] During construction, because all lanes of a road often are not paved at the same time, uneven construction quality (e.g., nonuniform compaction of asphalt pavements), construction techniques that allow some variation in the surface, and other factors may lead to different roughness measures for each lane.

[19] For two of the road segments, the nonmeasurable sections of road were left blank and the calculation of the final IRI used the value from the one measurable side of the road as the overall measure for that kilometer.

[20] MCC revised the original traffic targets for the Georgia, Vanuatu, and Armenia compacts. In Georgia and Vanuatu, MCC reduced traffic targets when it corrected the original baseline estimates. In Armenia, MCC increased the traffic target once the road project was placed on indefinite hold; the single road that MCC completed prior to the project hold had a higher traffic target than the full package of roads MCC originally planned to complete.

[21] MCC used a traffic count from a study conducted in 2005; however, construction of the road project began in 2006.

[22] In addition, the 2000 traffic study was conducted for a 72-kilometer section of highway, rather than the 18 kilometers designated for the project.

[23] MCC policy allows each country to determine the frequency and timing of each review, along with which indicators will be evaluated.

[24] The 2008 review provided several recommendations on how to structure the traffic count survey. In addition, a 2009 review found that the Vanuatu compact was at risk of double counting vehicles and recommended that the monitoring and evaluation plan indicate that traffic refers to the sum of the average number of vehicles passing over checkpoints.

[25] Third-party funding is funding from a source other than MCC or the partner government.

[26] MCC originally planned to fund all reconstruction included in the four sections of the Honduras highway project. However, because estimated costs had increased, MCC determined that it would be unable to complete all four sections within the 5-year compact timeframe and within the funding allocation. As a result, MCC funded about 94 percent of construction on sections 3 and 4, funded 31 percent of section 2, and funded none of section 1. The third-party funding from the Central American Bank of Economic Integration funded the difference. For more information on this project, see GAO-11-728.

[27] Phase 2 works included the expansion of Wharf 1 and construction of a new breakwater.

[28] While the project was largely completed as planned, components for a proposed fourth lot—which included a storage facility for dry bulk goods such as grains and sand and a fish quality inspection station—were deemed not viable once MCA-Benin conducted its feasibility studies. As a result, MCA-Benin did not tender a bid for that lot. According to MCC officials, the funds originally planned for those items were shifted to the other infrastructure components. The funds also helped cover cost increases and additional work on the wharf such as increasing wall length and dredging the berth.

[29] Reviews also identified other port indicators for improvement in Benin. For example, the 2008 and 2009 reviews indicated that the average duration of stay of trucks at port, which measures the reduction in time necessary for vehicles to cross the port due to reduced congestion, had a baseline value that was set with no justification of its actual level. The review recommended that this information be collected in the annual survey of port user satisfaction. MCA-Benin did so and determined that the baseline value was 7 hours. However, no changes were made to the final monitoring and evaluation plan to reflect this and MCC and MCA officials indicated that they agreed not to revise indicator baselines at the time.

[30] See GAO, *Millennium Challenge Corporation: Independent Review and Consistent Approaches Will Strengthen Projections of Program Impact*, GAO-08-730 (Washington, D.C.: Jun. 17, 2008).

[31] According to *Standards for Internal Control in the Federal Government*, a variety of control activities should be used in information processing, including checking the data entered. In addition, GAO's *Internal Control Management and Evaluation Tool* states that data validation and editing should be performed to identify erroneous data, which need to be reported and promptly corrected (GAO, *Internal Control Management and Evaluation Tool,* GAO-01-1008G (Washington, D.C.: August 2001).

[32] MCC officials told us that the original number of 53,988 beneficiaries was erroneous and should have been 111,442, in accordance with the 2004 Georgian Agricultural Census.

[33] The 2002 census indicates 6,769,914 for the population of Benin; adjusting population growth for 3 years leads to 7,419,235, not 8,490,000, in 2005. In addition, the supporting document that accompanied the beneficiary scrub spreadsheet and explained the computations had a different "original" baseline number—8,791,832—for 2005.

[34] MCC officials indicated that the standard time horizon for the beneficiary analysis is generally 20 years but that exceptions exist.

[35] In the case of Benin and Nicaragua, the growth rate for the year 2000 was added to the formula.

End Notes for Appendix I

[1] GAO-11-728. [2] GAO-12-630.

[3] We began work for this report in 2010; however, the job was suspended while we conducted work for a related engagement.

End Notes for Appendix II

[1] The statutory 5-year maximum timeframe begins once a compact enters into force.

In: Millennium Challenge Corporation
Editors: Justin Lane and Joseph Dunn
ISBN: 978-1-62808-184-8

Chapter 2

MILLENNIUM CHALLENGE CORPORATION: GEORGIA AND BENIN TRANSPORTATION INFRASTRUCTURE PROJECTS VARIED IN QUALITY AND MAY NOT BE SUSTAINABLE*

United States Government Accountability Office

WHY GAO DID THIS STUDY

MCC was established in 2004 to help developing countries reduce poverty and stimulate economic growth through multiyear compact agreements. As of June 2012, MCC had signed 26 compacts totaling about $9.3 billion in assistance. Seven compacts, including those with Georgia and Benin, closed in 2010 or 2011. Most had a transportation infrastructure project (a road or a port) that received about 50 percent of the compact's total funding. This report, prepared in response to a congressional mandate to review compact results, examines how MCC ensured the quality and sustainability of MCC's two transportation infrastructure projects in Georgia and Benin. GAO analyzed MCC documents, interviewed MCC officials and stakeholders, and observed the transportation infrastructure projects in those countries.

* This is an edited, reformatted and augmented version of United States Government Accountability Office, Publication No. GAO-12-630, dated June 2012.

WHAT GAO RECOMMENDS

To ensure that compact projects are implemented to established quality standards, GAO recommends that MCC (1) review how it uses information from its independent engineers, and (2) develop a mechanism to maintain influence on contractor repairs after compact closure. To ensure sustainability of compact projects, GAO recommends that MCC evaluate the tools it uses to ensure that partner countries have adequate resources to operate and maintain MCC-funded infrastructure. MCC agreed with all three recommendations but did not commit to taking any actions to address them.

WHAT GAO FOUND

In Georgia, quality and sustainability issues jeopardize the long-term usefulness of the Samtskhe-Javakheti road project. The Millennium Challenge Corporation (MCC) funded the rehabilitation of about 217 kilometers of road linking the previously isolated Samtskhe-Javakheti region with Tbilisi, the country's capital, and reducing the driving time from 8 1/4 hours to 2 3/4 hours. The project was intended to increase exports from the region, integrate people in the region with the rest of Georgia, and expand trade with Turkey and Armenia. However, the urgency to meet fixed time frames resulted in problems implementing the project's quality assurance framework. For example, the construction supervisor did not have enough staff to properly monitor construction and ensure quality. Despite several recommendations from MCC's independent engineer, MCC and its Georgian counterpart, the Millennium Challenge Account (MCA-Georgia), did not adequately increase the number of construction supervisors, which resulted in pavement defects in parts of 5 of the 11 road sections and deterioration of structures such as drainage and retaining walls. One 15-kilometer section contained enough defects that the road had to be completely repaved. Furthermore, much of the repair work was to be done in the contracts' 1-year defects liability period, after the compact closed and at a time when MCC no longer had oversight authority. Although MCC took steps to ensure the road project's sustainability, the Georgian government has demonstrated limited ability to keep the road operational and maintained.

In Benin, construction for the Port of Cotonou project generally met established quality standards, but several components were not in operation at the compact's end. MCC funded the construction of several port infrastructure improvements, including a jetty, a wharf, internal port roads, a railway, and security and electricity distribution systems. The project was intended to increase the efficient transport and volume of goods flowing through the port. However, several components—including the new south wharf, the port security system, and the electricity distribution system—were not in operation at compact completion because the Port Authority had not ensured that the necessary infrastructure, staffing, or policies were in place to operate them. For example, the new south wharf, which was intended to increase the cargo tonnage moving through the port, is not in operation in part because the Port Authority does not have the funds to complete the dredging needed to allow large vessels to access the new wharf. Even though MCC took steps to ensure that the government of Benin could sustain the operations and maintenance of the project—such as conducting a feasibility study, incorporating conditions precedent into the compact, hiring a port advisor, requiring a compact closure plan, and identifying steps the government of Benin should take to support sustainability in the compact letter of completion—they were not sufficient. As a result, Benin's inability to supply the resources, manpower, or policies needed to operate all of the port's components calls into question whether the port project will achieve expected compact results or be sustained throughout the life of the infrastructure.

ABBREVIATIONS

CEO	chief executive officer
IRI	International Roughness Index
ISPS	International Ship and Port Facility Security
km	kilometer
MCA	Millennium Challenge Account
MCC	Millennium Challenge Corporation
SOLAS	International Convention for the Safety of Life at Sea

June 27, 2012
The Honorable Patrick Leahy
Chairman

The Honorable Lindsey Graham
Ranking Member
Subcommittee on the Department of State,
Foreign Operations, and Related Programs
Committee on Appropriations
United States Senate

The Honorable Kay Granger
Chairwoman

The Honorable Nita Lowey
Ranking Member
Subcommittee on State, Foreign Operations,
and Related Programs
Committee on Appropriations
House of Representatives

The Millennium Challenge Corporation (MCC), a U.S. government corporation, was established in 2004 to provide aid to developing countries that have demonstrated a commitment to ruling justly, encouraging economic freedom, and investing in people. MCC provides assistance to eligible countries through multiyear compact agreements to fund programs targeted at reducing poverty and stimulating economic growth. MCC compacts may not be longer than 5 years.[1] As of June 2012, MCC had signed 26 compacts with 25 countries, committing a total of approximately $9.3 billion in U.S. funding.[2]

In the fiscal year 2008 Consolidated Appropriations Act, Congress directed GAO to review the results achieved by MCC compacts.[3] Seven of the 26 compacts were completed in 2010 or 2011, including those with the Republic of Georgia and Benin.[4] All 7 compacts included a transportation infrastructure project (a road or a port) which—except in the case of Armenia—received 50 percent or more of the compact's total funding. In response to the congressional mandate, this report examines the quality and sustainability of MCC's transportation infrastructure projects in Georgia and Benin. GAO has previously reviewed other compact results and found that insufficient planning, escalation of construction costs, and insufficient MCC review led to project delays, scope changes, and cost increases. We made recommendations to address the need for better planning and design.[5] To improve planning and designs, MCC has committed specific funds and has increased the length of time between compact signature and project implementation. MCC developed the compacts with Georgia and Benin before it revised these practices.

To assess the quality and sustainability of the two MCC-funded transportation infrastructure projects in Georgia and Benin, we analyzed U.S. agency documents and observed project results in both countries. We interviewed MCC officials in Washington, D.C., and MCC and Millennium Challenge Account (MCA) officials in Georgia and Benin regarding the results of the transportation infrastructure activities, including their quality and sustainability.[6] We also met with partner country government officials, contractors, project managers, construction supervisors, and relevant private businesses. We based our assessment of the projects' quality on observations of defects in a site visit to the projects, a review of reports provided by MCC, interviews of officials, and the quality assurance framework established by MCC, MCA, and their contractors. For this report, the definition of sustainability is based on the Organisation for Economic Cooperation and Development definition, which defines "sustainability" as "the continuation of benefits from a development intervention (such as assets, skills, facilities, or improved services) after major development assistance has been completed." We operationalized this definition by specifying that sustainability is the ability of MCC's partner country government to operate and maintain the new infrastructure in such a condition as is required to produce the projected benefits for the period of time those benefits are expected.

MCC enters into a legal relationship with partner country governments that vests responsibility for day-to-day management of compact project implementation to the MCA, including monitoring and evaluation activities such as setting and revising targets, but such MCA actions require MCC's direct oversight and approval. Therefore, throughout this report, we attribute all decisions related to project rescoping and compact targets to MCC. See appendix I for further details on our objectives, scope, and methodology.

We conducted this performance audit from November 2011 to June 2012 in accordance with generally accepted government auditing standards. Those standards require that we plan and perform the audit to obtain sufficient, appropriate evidence to provide a reasonable basis for our findings and conclusions based on our audit objectives. We believe the evidence obtained provides a reasonable basis for our findings and conclusions based on our audit objectives.

BACKGROUND

MCC Organization

MCC is managed by a chief executive officer (CEO), appointed by the President with the advice and consent of the Senate, and is overseen by a Board of Directors. The Secretary of State serves as board chair and the Secretary of the Treasury serves as vice-chair.[7] MCC's model is based on a set of core principles deemed essential for effective development assistance, including good governance, country ownership, focus on results, and transparency.

According to MCC, country ownership of an MCC compact occurs when a country's national government controls the prioritization process during compact development, is responsible for implementation, and is accountable to its domestic stakeholders for decision making and results.

In keeping with the MCC principle of country ownership, MCC enters into a legal relationship with partner country governments. During the 5-year compact implementation period, the partner government vests responsibility for day-to-day management, including monitoring and evaluation of the progress of compact projects, to an accountable entity established to implement the compact (an entity's name is usually formed from "MCA" plus the country's name—for example, MCA-Benin). MCC provides the framework and guidance for compact implementation, monitoring, and evaluation that MCAs are to use in implementing compact projects.

Following the compact end date, the partner government must close the program within 120 days (the closure period).

During the closure period, MCC funds may be used only for project goods, works, or services incurred before the compact end date, or for closure expenses. For example, the government may expend MCC funds to settle final invoices and claims, secure unfinished project sites against potential health or safety hazards, prepare final reports, and conduct other activities specified in MCC's closeout guidelines.

However, the government may not expend MCC funds to undertake or continue activities that were planned for completion within the compact term, including expenses for activities such as completion of works, supervising engineer services, and consulting services.

Quality Assurance Framework

MCC places several requirements on MCAs to ensure proper management and quality assurance of MCC-funded infrastructure projects. These requirements create a quality assurance framework for infrastructure projects that requires that each MCA have an individual project director—for example, a roads director—who oversees the activities of the other actors, including outside implementing entities or project management consultants, construction supervisors, and construction contractors.[8]

- *Project management consultant/implementing entity*: Before receiving project funding, MCC requires the MCAs to engage the services of a project management firm or an implementing entity to help manage administrative aspects of compact projects.
- *Construction supervisor:* MCAs contract with construction supervisors to conduct oversight of day-to-day construction and the activities of the construction contractors to ensure compliance with contract requirements. Construction supervisors play an important role in ensuring construction quality by performing such tasks as approving construction materials, overseeing testing, and inspecting completed work.
- *Construction contractor:* MCAs contract with construction firms to build the project. The construction contractor is also responsible for controlling the quality of its work, which involves, among other tasks, material and construction testing.[9]

In general, MCAs deliver infrastructure projects through a design-bid-build approach in which the MCA contracts with a design engineer to develop technical plans and specifications that are used by a construction contractor, hired under a separate MCA procurement action, to build the project. In some cases, project designs already exist and MCAs do not engage a design engineer in implementing the project. In other cases a design-build approach is used and MCA contracts with a contractor that becomes responsible for both project design and construction.

In addition, MCC may hire an independent engineer to assist in overseeing the progress of construction as managed by the MCAs and executed by their contractors. The objective of engaging an independent engineer is to obtain high-quality technical support in order to strengthen MCC's ability to better assess the quality of ongoing program activities and to make better informed judgments about the status of ongoing activities, particularly where assessment of project activities affects MCC's ability to further disburse funds. An independent engineer may also provide technical input on program decisions and documents submitted by MCC partner-country counterparts and help MCC ensure that funds are being spent according to the conditions and frameworks established in the compact. Figure 1 depicts the oversight, management, and contractual relationships among MCC, the MCA, and their contractors for infrastructure projects.

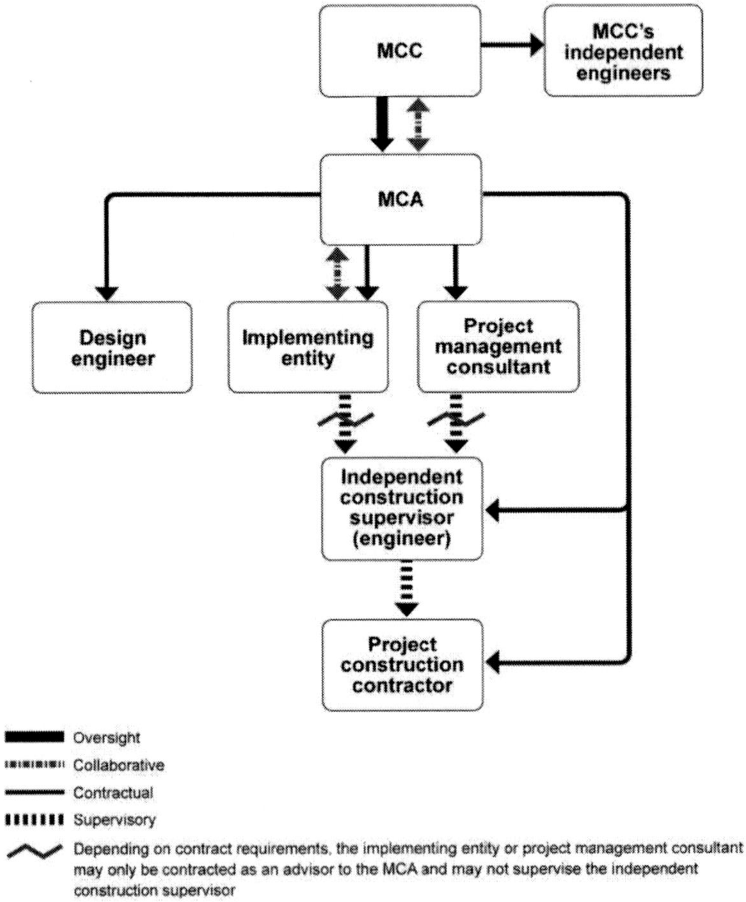

Source: GAO interpretation of contract and project management structures for large infrastructure projects.

Figure 1. MCC's Contract Management Structure for Infrastructure Projects.

Sustainability of MCC Projects

MCC takes steps to ensure the sustainability of the projects it funds during both the design and implementation phases. First, MCC compacts are to be designed so that projects are sustainable for about 20 years, or as appropriate for the structure. Also, during the compact development process, MCC assesses the mechanisms in place to enhance sustainability, including a partner country's policies and practices that will enable MCC investments to continue to provide benefits. For instance, as part of compact proposals submitted to MCC, partner countries are required to identify risks to project sustainability and describe the measures needed to ensure that project benefits can be sustained beyond the period of MCC financing. Partner countries are to consider a number of issues affecting sustainability, including environmental sustainability; institutional capacity for operations and maintenance; and, for proposed infrastructure projects, recent funding, performance, and expected expenses for operations and maintenance.

During compact implementation, MCC tracks progress against key policy reforms and institutional improvements that were included as conditions in the compact to enhance project impact and sustainability. Such conditions in an agreement are known as conditions precedent, which must be met by one party before a second party to the agreement can perform or do its part. In the case of an MCC compact, MCC establishes conditions precedent that must be met by the partner government or MCA before financial disbursements are made. For example, MCC may require that the government increase its budget allocation for road maintenance before releasing final payments.

Transportation Infrastructure Projects

For the purposes of this report, transportation infrastructure comprises public works that provide the conveyance of passengers or goods from one place to another. It includes structures such as roads, seaports, airports, and railways. Such projects may take years to plan and implement. For example, typical highway projects in the United States can take from 10 to 15 years for planning, design, and construction.

Transportation infrastructure construction contracts may contain a defects liability clause that obligates a contractor to repair or rectify defects in the construction for a set period after the construction supervisor has deemed the works substantially complete.[10] In a construction agreement, a contractor's main obligation is to carry out the works to final completion, free of defects and to the standard set out in the agreement. A defects liability clause is intended to supplement this obligation by ensuring that the contractor remedies any defective work that becomes noticeable during the defects liability period, usually 1 year. The clause also provides a mechanism for repairing defects that may arise during the defects liability period.

In Georgia, Quality and Sustainability Issues Jeopardize the Long-Term Usefulness of the SamtskheJavakheti Road Project

In Georgia, MCC funded the rehabilitation of about 217 kilometers[11] of road linking the previously isolated Samtskhe-Javakheti region with Tbilisi, the country's capital.[12] However, the urgency to meet fixed time frames resulted in problems implementing the quality assurance framework and led to construction defects in parts of 5 of the 11 road lots.[13] Furthermore, while MCC took steps to ensure the road project's sustainability, the Georgian government has demonstrated limited ability to keep the road operational and maintained up to this point.

MCC Compact Funded the Rehabilitation of the Samtskhe-Javakheti Road in Georgia

MCC signed a compact with the Republic of Georgia in September 2005 to stimulate growth in regions outside Tbilisi where more than 40 percent of the country's total population resides. A rough asphalt road before the compact, the Samtskhe-Javakheti Road was in such disrepair it prevented residents in the region from easily reaching Tbilisi. The purpose of the rehabilitation was to improve transportation for regional trade to

- increase exports from the region;
- increase social, political, and economic integration of the people in the region with those in the rest of Georgia;
- expand international trade by providing a more direct link from Tbilisi and eastern and southern Georgia to Turkey and Armenia;[14] and

- develop the tourism potential of Vardzia, a 13th century rock-cut monastery.

MCC originally granted $295.3 million for the compact's two projects—Enterprise Development and Regional Infrastructure Rehabilitation, which included the Samtskhe-Javakheti Roads Rehabilitation activity (see fig. 2).[15] In November 2008, after Georgia's war with Russia over South Ossetia, MCC increased the compact by $100 million. The compact entered into force in April 2006 and ended in April 2011.

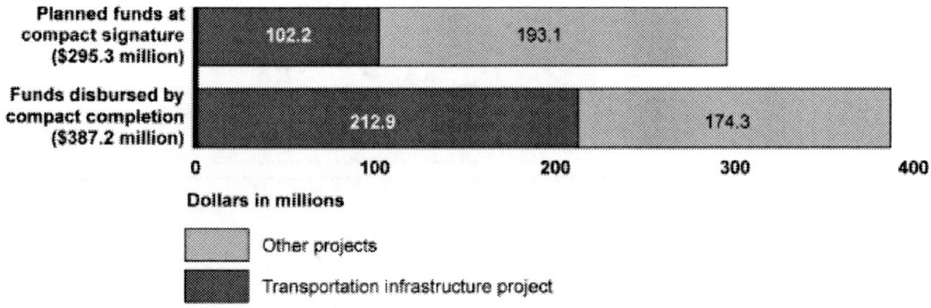

Source:

Note: MCC added $100 million to the compact in November 2008 after Georgia's war with Russia. Other projects include funds disbursed before entry into force to facilitate the implementation of the compact. At compact close, $8.1 million remained undisbursed.

Figure 2. MCC-Georgia Compact Funding at Signature and at Completion.

MCC originally planned to rehabilitate 245 kilometers of existing road at a cost of $102.2 million (or $417,000 per kilometer), but after several changes to the project's scope, rehabilitated about 217 kilometers at a cost of about $212.9 million (or $981,000 per kilometer). The road project's length was first reduced after the initial contract solicitation attracted bids that exceeded the amount of funding originally available for the road work. As a result, the project was divided into shorter sections and contracts were let for about 170 kilometers of road. In the winter of 2008-2009, after MCA-Georgia allocated an additional $60 million to the road project, about 50 kilometers of road were added to the project (see fig. 3). MCA-Georgia also reallocated an additional $50.7 million from other activities to the road project between May 2008 and January 2011 to cover additional cost increases, including costs to accelerate work to ensure its completion before the end of the compact.[16]

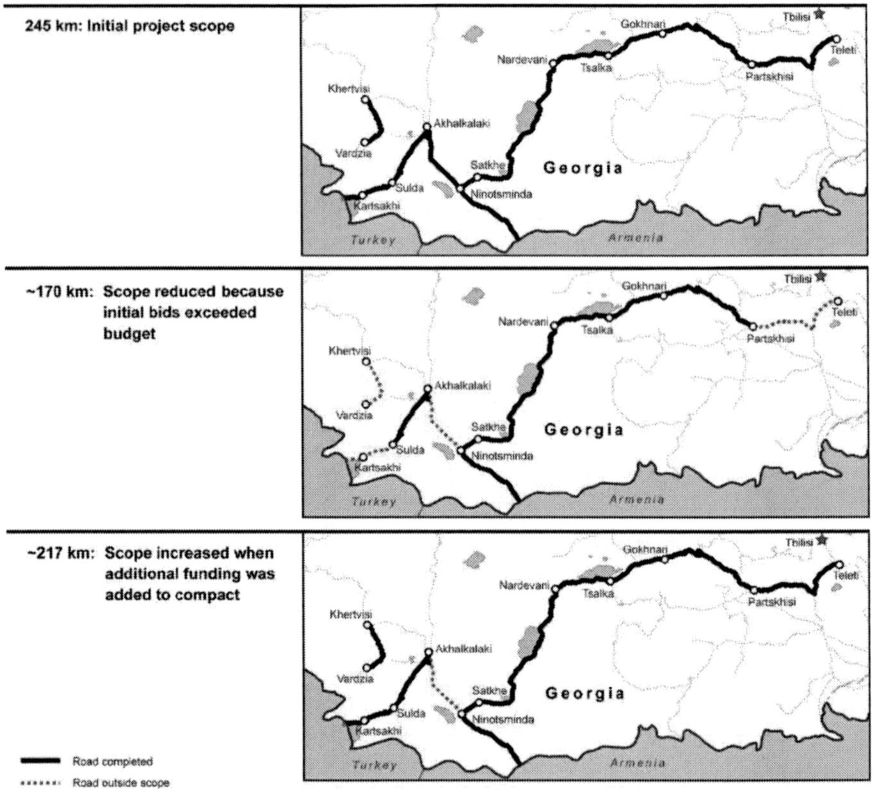

Source: GAO analysis of MCC and Republic of Georgia's government data, and Map Resources (maps).

Figure 3. Scope Changes for the Samtskhe-Javakheti Roads Rehabilitation Project.

The Urgency to Meet Compressed Construction Time Frames Resulted in Problems Implementing the Quality Assurance Framework and Construction Defects in 5 of the 11 Road Lots

The road was rehabilitated at an increased cost in a compressed construction time frame because of insufficient planning, work added late in the compact, and poor performance by one contractor. Because of the compressed construction time frames, MCA-Georgia's construction supervision and construction contractors had difficulty fully implementing the quality assurance framework. In addition, problems identified by MCC's independent engineer were not adequately addressed. As a result, repair work remained at the end of the compact and the quality of construction varied across the lots. Although some infrastructure, such as the bridges, appeared to be well built, parts of 5 of the 11 lots— representing about 60 percent of the kilometers rehabilitated—had noticeable pavement deterioration and other defective structures. The extent of the defects varied among the lots, with some lots requiring pavement surface sealing or a relatively small amount of patching. However, the road in one lot was planned to be entirely repaved. As of March 2012, work was ongoing. (Figure 4 shows how the road was divided into lots and handled by different contractors.)

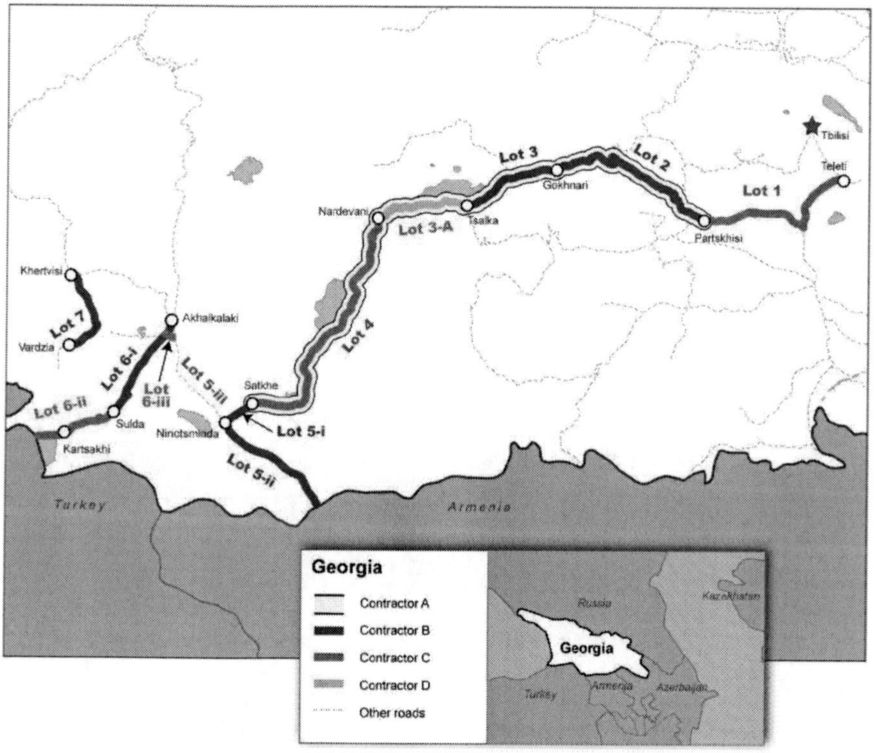

Source: GAO analysis of MCC and Republic of Georgia's government data, and Map Resources (maps).

Figure 4. Division of the Samtskhe-Javakheti Roads Rehabilitation Project into Lots.

Road Was Rehabilitated at Increased Cost under Compressed Construction Time Frames because of Several Factors

MCA-Georgia awarded most of the final construction contracts with 2 years or less before the compact end date because of planning delays, work added late in the compact, and poor performance by one contractor. See figure 5 for a timeline of the compressed time frame under which the road rehabilitation occurred.

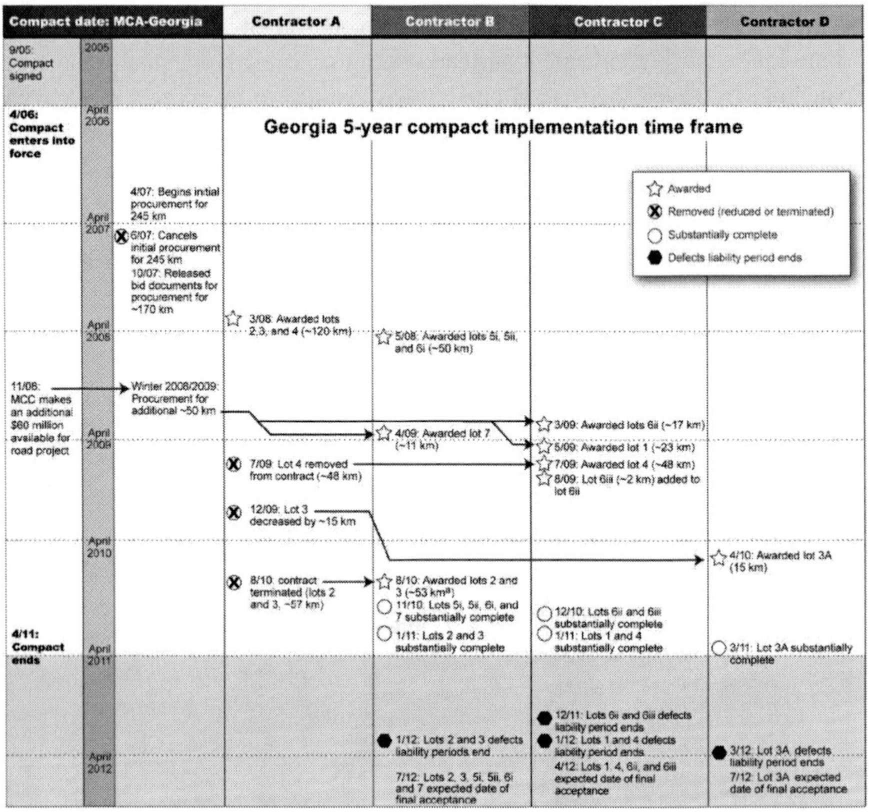

Source: GAO analysis of MCC and MCA-Georgia documents and interviews.

Note: Contractor A lot lengths were as of the time the event occurred, Contractors B, C, and D lot lengths were as of the end of the compact. Individual lot lengths may not add to total lengths because of rounding.

[a] When lot 3 was awarded to contractor A, it included work later re-awarded as lot 3A as well as 4 kilometers of road at Tsalka that were eventually removed from the project altogether.

Figure 5. Georgia Construction Timeline.

Insufficient planning delayed construction: MCC reports that conducting feasibility studies and preparing designs and bid documents took over a year of compact time. In addition, a lack of accurate cost estimates resulted in a delay of 8 to 10 months in the first contract's award. In April 2007, MCA-Georgia made its initial procurement for two road contracts and found that the project cost was greater than estimated and exceeded the funds available for the road work. 17 As a result, it removed about 75 kilometers from the scope, revised the project into smaller lots, conducted a new procurement, and awarded contracts for lots 2, 3, and 4 (about 120 kilometers total) to contractor A in March 2008 and for lots 5i, 5ii, and 6i (about 50 kilometers total) to contractor B in May 2008—23 and 25 months after the compact entered into force, respectively.

New work was added when additional funding became available late in the compact implementation period: In November 2008, MCC made additional funds available for the road project. The following spring, 3 years after the compact entered into force, MCA-Georgia awarded three additional road contracts (lots 1, 6ii, 18 and 7). At this point, only about 2 years remained under the compact to complete the work.

Poor performance by one contractor delayed implementation by about a year: Contractor A failed to meet its contractual obligations. After removing segments from contractor A's scope of work in July and December 2009 and awarding them to other contractors, MCA-Georgia terminated the contract in August 2010. While reassigning the work from contractor A to the other contractors allowed the contract to be completed before the end of the compact, MCC officials reported that the process cost MCA-Georgia about $45 million more than the original $65 million contract and added at least 1 year of construction time.

MCA-Georgia provided a notice of nonperformance to contractor A in April 2009. That July, MCA-Georgia removed lot 4 from the contract (48 kilometers) and awarded it to another contractor through a limited procurement process. By using the quicker limited procurement process, MCA-Georgia hoped to take advantage of time remaining in the 2009 construction season and improve the likelihood of getting the work completed in the 21 months remaining in the compact.

- In December 2009, contractor A's performance was still a problem, and MCA-Georgia removed an additional 15 kilometers from the contract (lot 3A). According to MCC officials, MCA-Georgia re-awarded this work through a full, competitive procurement process. As a result, the procurement took more than 4 months, mostly over the winter season, which left about 1 year to complete the work.

- In August 2010, MCC terminated the contract with contractor A for the remaining 57 kilometers of road (work for this section was about 80 percent complete, according to MCC's independent engineer). With only 8 months left before the compact was to end—and most of those being winter months—MCA-Georgia removed about 4 kilometers from the project and re-awarded the other 53 kilometers using a limited procurement process so that work could begin immediately. According to MCC, MCA-Georgia paid contractor B $31.8 million to complete the work before the compact's April 2011 deadline. An independent adjudicator found the additional cost for completing the work to be within the bounds of what may reasonably be expected in such circumstances.

Quality Assurance Problems Identified by MCC's Independent Engineer Not Always Addressed

The MCC-required quality assurance framework was in place, but issues identified by MCC's independent engineer—the technical advisor MCC hired to assist in overseeing the progress of construction—were not always addressed. Specifically, the contractors did not always perform their quality control responsibilities, the construction supervision firm had insufficient staff to conduct its work, and MCA-Georgia did not always use the construction supervisor as set out in the quality assurance framework.

Contractors did not always conduct quality control activities: The contractors did not always fulfill their contractual quality control role, according to MCC officials and MCC's independent engineer's reports. For example, MCC's independent engineer reported that some contractors continued work in less-than-favorable conditions, such as cold and rainy weather, to complete the work before the end of the compact. Conducting work in these conditions can cause problems with curing concrete (such that it does not reach its design strength) or with asphalt raveling (not bonding to other asphalt layers). In addition, to meet time frames, much work was completed at night when poor lighting, less inspection, and colder temperatures made it more difficult to perform high-quality work. Finally, one contractor did not supply a required quality assurance plan.[19] Without the contractor's quality assurance plan for the specific contract, the construction supervisor did not know when the contractor would be testing materials or who to contact regarding identified problems. In addition, the same contractor turned in test reports after the tested work had already been covered by subsequent stages of work. As a result, if the construction supervisor found that the earlier work was defective, the contractor would have to remove the subsequent work to repair it.

Construction supervisor had insufficient staff: Quality control errors by the contractors should have been caught by the construction supervisor, but the construction supervisor had insufficient numbers of staff to adequately implement the quality assurance framework, according to MCC's independent engineer. MCA-Georgia did increase the contract supervision, but not to the independent engineer's recommended level. While MCC had taken steps to try to ensure sufficient supervision of the construction, it did not have authority to enforce the independent engineer's recommendations.

- MCC's independent engineer, accompanied by MCC officials, visited the road project and provided written reports almost quarterly between February 2009 and November 2010—the compressed construction time frames under which most of the roadwork occurred. The reports stated that there were not enough construction supervision staff, and, in four of those reports, the independent engineer advised that the supervisory situation was jeopardizing the project's quality and success. A project management official told us that, because of the insufficient number of staff, the construction supervisor did not observe some quality testing that was done by the construction contractors, as required in its contract.
- In February 2009, MCA-Georgia increased the number of construction supervision staff to oversee the three lots added to the project's scope.[20] In addition, MCA-Georgia hired a separate construction supervisor to oversee lot 3A when it was created, increasing the staff available overall for construction supervision on the project. However, the MCC independent engineer recommended that additional construction staff were still needed to ensure the quality of the work under way. The independent engineer also reported that the construction supervisory firm's fee was lower than typical for this type of international work.[21] Nonetheless, MCA-Georgia chose not to fund additional staff for the construction supervision firm.
- MCC had included a condition precedent in the compact that required MCA-Georgia to engage a construction supervisor. However, because the condition was satisfied once MCA-Georgia engaged a supervisor, MCC stated that the condition precedent did not give it any authority to withhold funds because of insufficient supervision staffing.

Construction supervisor was not always used in accordance with the quality assurance framework: According to two reports by MCC's independent engineer, MCA-Georgia did not always use the construction supervision staff effectively. According to the quality control framework in the construction firms' contracts, the construction supervisor should issue all instructions to the contractors. However, MCC's independent engineer noted that the MCA-Georgia staff responsible for the road project communicated directly with construction contractors and issued oral instructions directly to the contractors to accelerate work. The independent engineer further noted that this practice could lead to claims of additional work, increasing costs, because contractors received different instructions from the construction supervisor and MCA-Georgia.

Road Was Improved, but Quality Problems Exist in the Pavement and Some Structures

The MCC project generally improved the road by reducing its driving time and roughness and installing bridges that appeared well built. However, several sections of the road had pavement defects and structures such as drainage systems and retaining walls that are deteriorating.

MCC Project Created Improved Road and Bridges

The MCC project improved the condition of the road. Before rehabilitation, the Samtskhe-Javakheti road was passable but rough, with a driving time of about 81/4 hours. The project decreased the road's roughness, and after rehabilitation, the same trip could be made in about 23/4 hours. MCC reported roughness measurements before rehabilitation that indicated a vehicle would have to drive under about 30 miles per hour for passengers to ride comfortably.[22] Road roughness measurements made after project completion indicated that passengers could ride comfortably even at speeds of 75 miles per hour. We traveled a portion of the road that was bypassed by the rehabilitation project and found it to be filled with potholes and patches. We found the new road was much smoother (see fig. 6).

The scope of the project also included rehabilitating or rebuilding 27 bridges (see fig. 7). In March 2012, MCC's independent engineer reported that all bridges were performing well and had only a few defects such as erosion of embankment slopes, and incomplete guardrail hardware. We observed only minor defects such as a small chip in a bridge beam but no apparent quality problems.

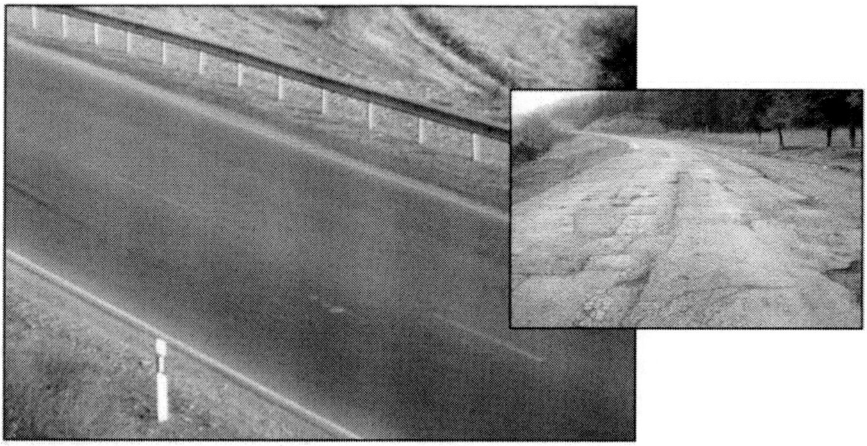

Source: GAO.

Figure 6. Example of the MCC-Funded Road, Lot 1 (Inset: Unrehabilitated Road Bypassed by MCC-Funded Road).

Source: GAO.

Figure 7. MCC-Funded Bridge in Lot 7.

Pavement Defects Occur in Parts of 5 of the 11 Road Lots

While the pavement in some lots appeared to be in good condition, the pavement in other lots was not. We observed that the pavement in road lots 1 and 7 was smooth with minimal defects. However, we found pavement deterioration in parts of 5 of the 11 road lots.[23] The amount of deterioration and completed repair work varied in those lots, which constituted about 60 percent of the total kilometers of the final project.

- In lots 4 and 6ii, surface deterioration had been treated with a surface sealer to keep the surface from deteriorating further (see fig. 8). While seal coating may keep water from entering the cracks and make the road look better in the short term, it does not add pavement strength. As a result, deterioration will continue under the anticipated increased traffic loads for the project if the underlying cause of the cracking is not repaired.

Source: GAO.

Figure 8. Seal Coat Repair on Center of Road in Lot 4.

- Lots 2 and 3 had undergone patching, but in one case the patch failed and the deterioration had continued beyond the patch, as shown in figure 9.
- In other places, we found continued cracking in need of repair, as shown in figure 10. This type of cracking—known as alligator cracking—is caused by fatigue failure of the asphalt surface, which is related to weakened layers of asphalt beneath the pavement, insufficient pavement thickness, excessive loading, or some combination of these factors.

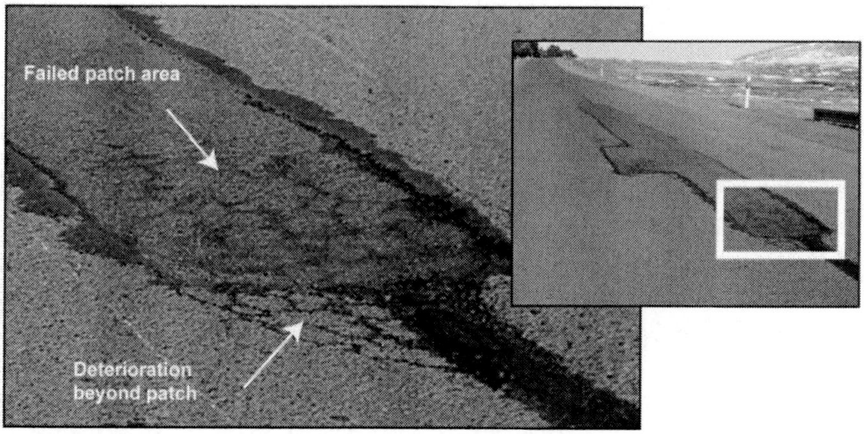

Source: GAO.

Figure 9. Failed Patch and Continued Deterioration in Lot 3.

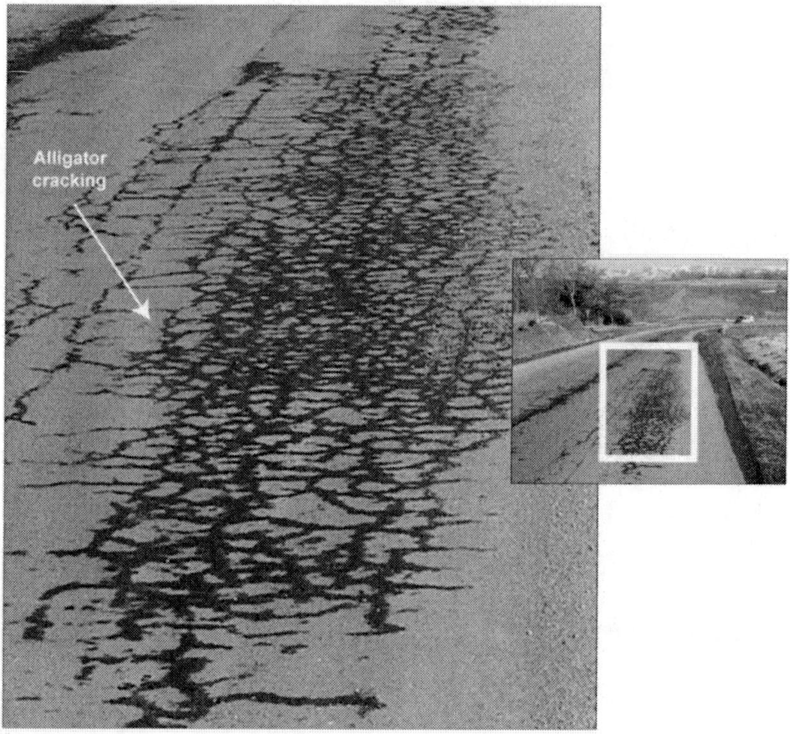

Source: GAO.

Figure 10. Additional Pavement Cracking in Lot 2.

- In lot 3A, much of the pavement was failing and under repair. The contractor was in the process of milling the top layer of pavement in some areas and full-depth patching of the pavement in other areas (see fig. 11). In June 2011, MCC's independent engineer noted that the entire lot 3A section of road (15 kilometers) had been constructed poorly and had moderate to severe levels of distress in the pavement, which indicated that a poor quality of asphalt had been used. The construction supervisor stated that the contractor paved the road in lot 3A in two layers and that the second layer was paved when the weather was rainy to complete the project on time. However, the second layer did not bond to the first and thus fell apart. According to the independent engineer, some portions of the road will require full-depth reconstruction of the road. A Georgian government official stated that the lot 3A contractor had agreed to replace the base materials in some places and repave the entire lot.

Source: GAO.

Figure 11. Pavement Milling and Patching Under Way in Lot 3A.

The construction supervisor's most recent (December 2011) list of pavement defects indicated pothole patching and surface dressing was needed for lots 2, 3, 3A, 5i, and 5ii. However the independent engineer's March 2012 trip report stated there were more extensive pavement defects that required correction measures such as pothole repair, surface dressing, crack repairs, or full-depth reconstruction for lots 1, 2, 3, 3A, 4, 5ii, 6ii, 6iii, and 7. The independent engineer also noted in several locations that the defects resulted from incorrectly repaired previous defects, the inadequate winter maintenance of the roads, and, in one section of road, traffic loads heavier than the road was designed to carry. The independent engineer also stated that if the roads are not correctly repaired, they will worsen. Defects not properly repaired will likely fail under increased traffic loads or further deteriorate, creating potholes as water enters the cracks in the winter and then freezes. On the basis of the independent engineer's assessment that some of the project contractors were not meeting contract specifications, MCC sent a letter to MCA-Georgia in September 2010, noting that the work methods on lots 2, 3, 3A, and 4 were not to the standards expected and that the base material and pavement compaction required immediate improvement. The letter also stated that if the contractors did not improve the work, it would not be accepted.

Some Drainage Structures and Retaining Walls Were Defective

Structures such as drains and retaining walls are critical to a road's longevity. A working drainage system helps to keep water off the road, which is critical to safety and to keep pavement from prematurely deteriorating. However, we found defects in the drainage systems of 7 of the 11 lots. For example:

- In lots 1, 5ii, 6i, 6ii, and 7, we found some of the drainage channels collapsing or cracked, which could cause the drains to become blocked (see fig. 12).

In lots 2, 6i, and 6ii, we found the concrete drainage channels with defects because of poor concrete construction (see fig. 13).

- In lots 3, 5i, and 5ii, drains were installed above the water level in some places, making it impossible for water to drain off the road (see fig. 14).

Source: GAO.

Figure 12. Defective Drain Tops.

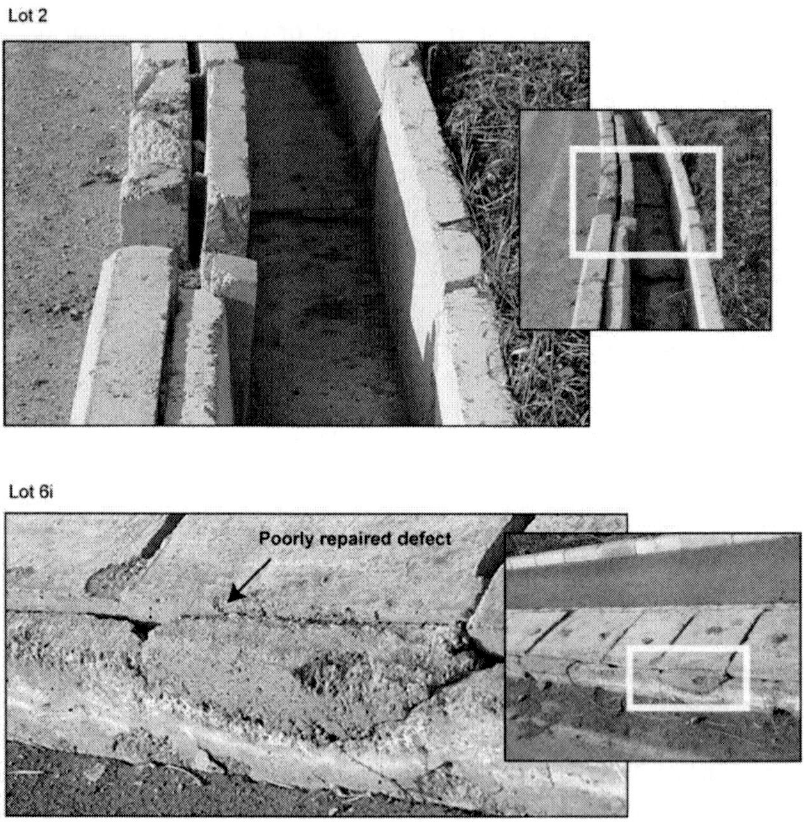

Source: GAO.

Figure 13. Drainage Channel Construction Defects in Lots 2 and 6i.

Source: The Louis Berger Group, Inc.

Figure 14. Drainage System Drain Holes Too High to Allow Water to Drain in Lot 3.

According to MCC's independent engineer, the quality of the drain placement and the construction of the tops were inadequate because the concrete did not cure properly or had already started to harden before it was poured.

If the drainage system does not work properly, the water will saturate and weaken the underlying ground and cause the road to deteriorate or freeze in the winter and create a safety hazard.

Furthermore, we observed a failed retaining wall that, if left unrepaired, could damage the road. Because the retaining wall had failed, serious erosion had occurred, and if the erosion continues, it will progress until it reaches the road, jeopardizing the road's future usefulness (see fig. 15).

We also found additional erosion in lots 2, 6ii, and 7 (for example, see fig. 16).

The independent engineer in his March 2012 report indicated a few erosion concerns for lots 2, 3, and 7 that needed to be corrected. The corrections are necessary for motorist safety and to protect the pavement, bridges, and retaining walls.

Source: GAO.

Figure 15. Failed Retaining Wall in Lot 2.

Source: GAO.

Figure 16. Erosion.

Work and Defects Remained after Compact End Date, but MCC Has No Authority to Ensure Their Completion and Repair

Although the construction supervisor certified the contracted road work as substantially complete by the end of the compact, the previously described construction defects had not been repaired. Once the work was certified as substantially complete, responsibility for the roads moved from the contractors to MCA-Georgia, and final contract payments with MCC funds were made. However, according to the contracts, contractors continue to be responsible for the completion of any work or defects related to work quality during a 1-year defects liability period. The transfer of the road lots to MCA-Georgia included a list of about 700 defects identified by the construction supervisor to be completed or repaired after substantial completion and before the end of the defects liability period (see table 1). Additional defects can be added to the list by the construction supervisor if they appear in the 1-year liability period. MCC officials stated that it is desirable to complete as much of the work as possible before the defects liability period starts. However, it was necessary to accept the work as substantially complete before the end of the compact time frame so that final MCC funds disbursement could be made to MCA-Georgia. As a result, the work that remained and the repair of the remaining defects were moved into the defects liability period.[24]

Table 1. Defects as of Substantial Completion by Lot

Lot	Number of defects
1	33
2	85
3	24
3A	70
4	128
5i[a]	43
5ii[a]	37
6i[a]	129
6ii	58
6iii	13
7	32
Other[a]	49
Total	701

Source: GAO analysis of MCC documents

[a] An additional 49 defects were listed on bridges on lots 5i, 5ii and 6i, which we could not attribute to a specific lot.

[b] Defects not attributable to a specific lot.

Additional factors present challenges to ensuring the defective work is adequately repaired:

- MCC's independent engineer reported in October 2011 that the repair work under way on lot 3A was not in accordance with standard procedures and that the road that had been patched was unsatisfactory. For example, the contractor did not apply sufficient bonding material to ensure that the layers of asphalt would adhere to each other before laying additional asphalt. In addition, the independent engineer commented that patch cutting and laying of asphalt were not properly done.
- We observed in December 2012 that much repair work remained to be done. In addition, during the summer construction season in 2011 no construction supervision firm was in place for about 2 months of August and September 2011. According to the October 2011 report of MCC's independent engineer, this may have affected the contractors' progress in rectifying construction defects. The gap in supervision occurred because the Georgian government contracted with a new construction supervisor for the defects liability period after the compact-funded construction supervisor's contract ended. The new construction supervisor provided us with a summary of defects remaining at the end of 2011, but it was not in the same format as the original defects list. It was thus impossible to determine which defects had been corrected and which had been added.

The Georgian government held performance guarantees from the contractors to ensure the work was completed.[25] However, correction of the work could not be completed in the 1-year defects liability period, and the independent engineer reported in March 2012 that the performance guarantees for lots 1, 4, 6ii, and 6iii had expired before the lots were accepted as complete. The independent engineer also reported the performance guarantees for lots 2, 3, 3A, 5i, 5ii, 6i, and 7 were extended until August 2012, after the expected date that those lots will be accepted.[26]

Although several officials in Georgia stated that the repairs will be made, MCC has little ability to ensure the work will be done or done correctly. MCC has little oversight ability to ensure the work is completed now that the compact has ended. For example:

- MCC reported that documentation regarding the status of the projects in the defects liability period is held by the Georgian government. While the Georgian government provided MCC the project status for 3 of the 11 lots as of April 2012, the documentation provided was not in English.
- MCC's independent engineer's last trip to Georgia to review the status of the project was in March 2012, just before its contract expired. MCC will have little technical assistance in determining the extent to which all quality issues were addressed through the planned end of all of the defects liability periods in July 2012. MCC stated that it is considering other arrangements to support a site inspection in June 2012.
- All funds have been paid to the Georgian government for the project, and the conditions precedent for the compact are no longer in force, such as requiring a project management consultant and a construction supervisor to be in place. MCC officials stated that they therefore have no authority to ensure the road is repaired appropriately before the Georgian government takes final acceptance of the roads and releases the funds retained to the contractors.

MCC Took Steps to Ensure Sustainability, but the Georgian Government Shows Limited Ability to Keep the Road Operational and Well Maintained

To sustain planned benefits such as reduced travel times and reduced user costs, Georgia will need to keep the road operational and maintain the pavement in good condition.[27] Before signing the compact, MCC took several steps to ensure that Georgia would be able to sustain the planned benefits of the rehabilitated road. However, we found that regular maintenance requirements, snow removal operations, and limited funds will challenge the Georgian government's ability to sustain MCC's investment in the road.

MCC Took Steps to Ensure Sustainability

MCC took steps to ensure sustainability by including conditions precedent in the compact and by funding some equipment for road maintenance.[28]

MCC officials stated that the Georgia compact included a condition precedent requiring the Georgian government to maintain a certain level of funding to ensure proper maintenance of the road during the compact.[29] MCC officials further stated that the condition precedent followed a similar requirement set in a World Bank loan agreement that had been entered into slightly earlier than the MCC compact, which emphasized ensuring that the government has the resources necessary to care for its national roads. MCC reported that, to sustain the economic opportunities generated by the road improvements, Georgia increased road maintenance funding from $33.6 million in 2006 to $56 million in 2010. In addition, MCC officials stated that the Roads Department of the Ministry of Regional Development and Infrastructure had been working with the World Bank to develop the institutional framework and technical capacity to provide good road maintenance. MCC officials also stated that they allowed MCA-Georgia to use funds left over at compact end to purchase some equipment (such as an excavator and a road-patching vehicle) that would help equip the Georgian road department to perform maintenance. Finally, MCC officials stated that Georgia, similar to other developing countries, will face difficult decisions in how it spends its money. They noted that the Georgian government has a preference for constructing new roads instead of maintaining old ones; however, they believed that Georgia would maintain the new road as a source of national pride and hoped that, by working with MCC and other infrastructure development partners such as the World Bank, the government had come to realize the value of maintaining its investments.[30]

Routine and Emergency Maintenance Not Done

During our visit to the road, we found that many maintenance items not covered under the contractors' defects liability period were not being done. For example, we found several lots where the pavement markings were worn and needed to be repainted, guardrails and concrete barrier walls had been damaged and not repaired, drainage systems needed repair, and erosion was filling the drainage system and had not been cleaned (see fig. 17).

The MCC independent engineer also noted in June 2011, October 2011, and again in March 2012 that routine maintenance seemed to be lacking on some lots, including cleaning drainage channels and culverts, repairing damaged guardrails, and repairing erosion spots, and other miscellaneous damages. A Georgian official stated that there were maintenance contracts in place to make these kinds of repairs, and the MCC independent engineer stated in March 2012, that it did find Georgian road department contractors performing some routine maintenance tasks, but additional efforts were needed, and that a lack of snow removal in the 2011-2012 winter had likely resulted in increased road deterioration.

Source: GAO.

Figure 17. Damaged Concrete Barrier Wall, Drainage Channel Needing Maintenance, and Erosion-Filled Drainage.

Lot 4 Is Subject to Road Closure because of Snow

The feasibility study for the road project noted that portions of lots 3, 4, 5ii, 6i, and 6ii are prone to snow drifts and part of lot 4 is sometimes closed from October to March. Snow removal is part of keeping the road operational. In its absence, the road is closed to traffic and the planned benefits of the improved road such as reduced user costs, reduced travel time to Tbilisi, and economic benefits from increased trade will not be fully realized.

In the curved areas of the road prone to icing, we saw small piles of salt and sand; however, we did not see snow removal equipment or any winter maintenance operations, even though the Georgian government officials stated they had maintenance contracts in place to provide snow removal operations. The project's feasibility study had recommended installing snow fences to minimize snow drifts on the road, but on the basis of environmental concerns, MCA-Georgia chose to plant trees (living snow fences) to stop the snow drifting across the road and reduce maintenance costs. However, many of these trees did not survive. Living snow fences take several years to provide effective snow control.

Snow-closed road.

Snow constricts road to one lane.

Source: GAO.

Figure 18. Snow on Roads in Lot 4.

During our December 2011 field work, we found that the road was closed in lot 4 for the 2 days we were on-site because of snow drifts on one short (about a quarter of a kilometer) portion of lot 4. The project included electronic message signs on the road leaving Tbilisi to allow motorists to choose an alternate route. In addition, we found other portions of lot 4 to have only one lane open to traffic (see fig. 18). The independent engineer's March 2012 trip report stated that the Georgian road department's snow removal operations had been lacking during the 2011- 2012 winter season, which had heavy and repeated snow storms. The engineers stated the road had been closed in lot 4 from December 2011 until they visited in March 2012 and they found other sections of the road with only narrow lanes open, resulting in traffic jams and minor accidents.

Available Maintenance Budget May Be Insufficient for Road Upkeep and Operation

The Georgian government may not have a sufficient maintenance budget to maintain and operate the road. A Georgian government official stated that it had about $63 million in its 2012 budget to maintain roads. This appears to be a decrease from previous years' road maintenance budgets ($81 million in 2011 and $90 million in 2010). However, this is still an increase over the $56 million MCC reported that it had budgeted in 2010 to fulfill a condition precedent in the compact. Furthermore, of the overall 2012 road maintenance budget, the government had budgeted about $720,000 for maintaining the MCC road specifically. However, this amount of funding may be insufficient because MCA-Georgia approved paying contractors almost $700,000 to provide winter snow removal for only part of the road (lots 2, 3, 3A, and 4) during the 2010-2011 winter.

Road Construction Defects Jeopardize Long-Term Sustainability

The road construction defects discussed above may increase maintenance costs, decrease the life span of the project, and result in reduced benefits from the project. Even if the road defects are adequately repaired, they could increase the cost of maintenance because of the need to seal cracks at the edges of pavement patches and reseal road surface treatments periodically to provide protection to the pavement. If not adequately repaired, the roads will need ongoing maintenance to keep them in such condition that they can provide benefits to the citizens of Georgia.

In Benin, Port Construction Is Generally Good Quality, but Full Operability of Port Components Is Uncertain

In Benin, MCC constructed several infrastructure improvements to the Port of Cotonou, including a jetty, a wharf, internal port roads, a railway, and security and electricity distribution systems. The project was intended to increase the efficient transport and volume of goods flowing through the port. At project completion, the quality of construction generally met established quality standards. However, several of the port's critical components were inoperable at the end of the compact, including the new south wharf, the port security system, and the electricity distribution system. The government of Benin's inability to supply the resources, manpower, or policies needed to operate all of the port's components calls into question whether the port project will meet expected compact results or be sustainable for the life of the infrastructure.

MCC Compact Funded Infrastructure Improvements to the Port of Cotonou in Benin

In February 2006, MCC signed a compact with Benin, providing $307 million for four projects—Access to Land, Financial Services, Justice, and Markets—to improve physical and institutional infrastructure and increase private sector activity and investment.[31] The Access to Markets activity, which accounted for just over $169 million, or 55 percent of the total compact funding, went to improve the Port of Cotonou's infrastructure, specifically to increase efficiency and the volume of goods flowing through the port. By the time the compact ended, the final cost of the infrastructure improvements increased to about $188 million, accounting for over 60 percent of the final compact amount (see fig. 19). The compact entered into force in October 2006 and ended in October 2011. The project components were awarded to construction contractors in a series of lots, as follows (see fig. 20):

- lot 1: jetty to slow the rate at which sand will fill the access channel;
- lot 2: south wharf, a new wharf intended to increase volume of goods;
- lot 3: east-west road, security, electricity distribution system, fire protection, and lighting; and

- lot 3A: bypass road, railway, boundary wall, truck parking lot, and lighting.

In addition, the MCC funds allowed the port to purchase oceanographic equipment, antipollution equipment, and a tugboat.

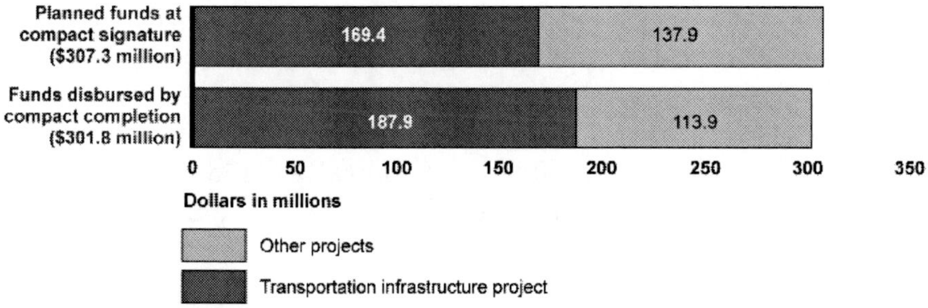

Source: GAO analysis of MCC data.

Note: Other projects include funds disbursed before entry into force to facilitate the implementation of the compact. At compact close, $5.5 million funds remained undisbursed.

Figure 19. MCC Benin Compact Funding at Signature and Completion.

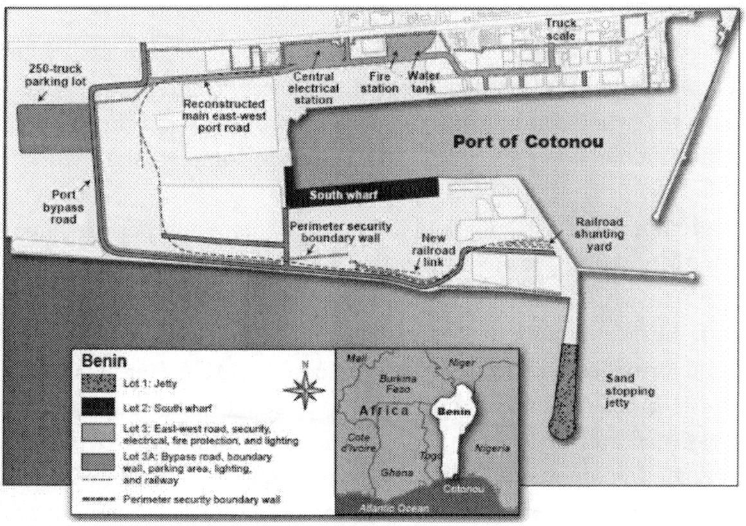

Source: GAO analysis of MCC data, Map Resources (map).

Figure 20. Compact-Funded Improvements in the Port of Cotonou. See Appendix II for additional information regarding Figure 20.

While the project was largely completed as planned, components for a proposed Lot 4—which included a storage facility for dry bulk goods such as grains and sand and a fish quality inspection station—were deemed not viable once MCA-Benin conducted its feasibility studies. As a result, MCA-Benin did not tender a bid for that lot. According to MCC officials, the funds originally planned for those items were shifted to the other infrastructure components. The funds also helped cover cost increases and additional work on the wharf such as increasing wall length and dredging the berth.[32]

The Quality of Construction Was Generally Good, but Many Defects Left for Repair or Minor Works to Be Completed after Compact Closure

MCC's two primary challenges in completing the port project were overcoming a late start to the construction, and managing the underperformance of one contractor. Despite these challenges, most of the infrastructure components had no or only minor quality issues. However, one lot had over 500 uncompleted tasks or defects when the compact closed.

Implementation Challenged by Delayed Start and One Underperforming Contractor

MCA-Benin did not sign contracts with its construction contractors until almost 3 years after the compact entered into force. During those years, MCA-Benin studied what components of the port project would be feasible. As a result, construction contractors had just 2 years to complete their work (see fig. 21).

In addition, MCA-Benin had to manage the poor performance of the contractor for lot 3 to get the project finished within the compact's time frame. According to MCC, the lot 3 contractor experienced internal management problems, missed important contract deadlines, did not perform contracted work, and provided inconsistent information to MCA-Benin and MCC. In August 2010, MCA-Benin terminated components of the contract, including the bypass road, railway, parking lot, and boundary wall. MCA-Benin awarded the terminated components as lot 3A to the contractor for the jetty that had been successful in meeting the time frames for the jetty component. After several extensions of time, the lot 3 contractor's remaining work was certified as substantially complete, months after the originally anticipated contract completion date and 1 day after the end of the compact. However, several components were left to be finished or corrected during the defects liability period.

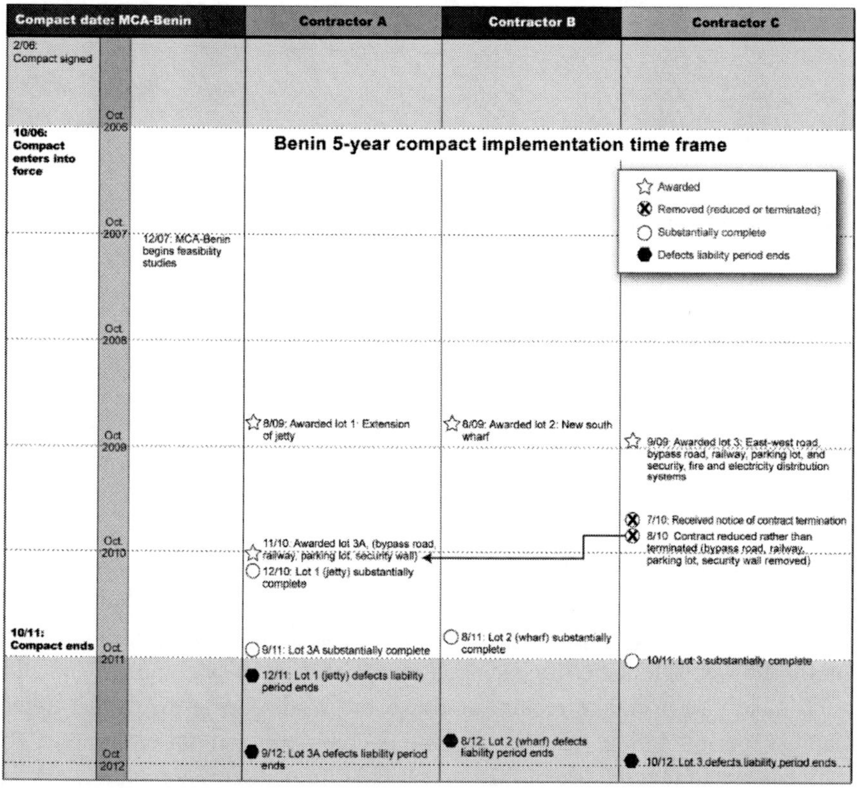

Source: GAO analysis of MCC and MCA-Benin documents and interviews.

Figure 21. Benin Construction Timeline.

Some Project Components Were Well Constructed, but One Lot Had Over 500 Problems

We found some of the project components to be completed and functioning for their intended use with only minor repairs needed during the defects liability period. For example, the lot 1 jetty was installed and reducing the amount of sand coming into the port from the ocean, thereby reducing periodic dredging maintenance costs (see fig. 22). We did observe that some areas of the jetty's concrete surface had small areas of cracking, which will require future maintenance.

Source: GAO.

Figure 22. Jetty Is Complete and Serving Its Intended Purpose.

The construction supervisor reported that some project components needed to be repaired or completed upon substantial completion of the contracts. However, because the construction supervisor deemed these issues minor, he was able to certify each contract as substantially complete and allow each contractor to make repairs or finish the work during the 1-year defects liability period following the substantial completion of the contract. MCC officials stated that the use of the defects liability period to complete work was not an ideal situation, but it was appropriate for situations in which the contractor needed to rely on an outside entity to complete the work (such as for the electricity distribution system) and in cases where the construction supervisor deemed the work to be minor.[33]

We observed some of these items during our field work and also concluded that they were generally minor in nature; however, lot 3 had over 500 items to be completed or corrected in the defects liability period (see table 2). As of April 2012, the project management consultant provided documentation that only 20 items remained to be completed and 5 items were listed as outstanding defects in lot 3. The consultant reported no uncompleted work or outstanding defects reported to be remaining from the takeover date on lots 1, 2, or 3A.

Table 2. Uncompleted Works and Outstanding Defects as of Substantial Completion, by Lot

Lot	Uncompleted work	Outstanding defects	Total
1	0	0	0
2	13	30	43
3	219	290	509
3A	4	120	124
Total	236	440	676

Source: GAO analysis of MCA-Benin construction supervisor documents.

Note: The lots' dates of substantial completion range from December 2010 to October 2011.

For lot 3, the construction supervisor reported that minor items needed to be completed or corrected included connecting the fire pump to the power supply, completing some paved areas, and installing a truck weigh station. In lot 3A, we also observed uncompleted work—such as lighting poles had not been completed in the 250-truck parking lot—and some minor defects needing repair—such as missing manhole covers in the road and a leaking pipe connecting the water tank to the fire control system (see fig. 23).

Source: GAO.

Figure 23. Lighting Pole under Construction.

MCC Took Steps to Ensure Sustainability, but Port Authority Has Not Been Able to Operate Key Project Components

Although MCC took steps to ensure the port project's sustainability, many of the project's key components—the south wharf, the security system, the electricity distribution system, and the fire station—were either not operational or only partially operational at the end of the compact. The south wharf had additional work remaining to be completed by the Port Authority and the concessionaire hired to operate the wharf for it to be functional, and the Port Authority had not ensured that all other necessary infrastructure and staffing were in place for the security system, the electricity distribution system, and the fire station.

MCC Took Steps to Ensure Sustainability

MCC took several steps to ensure that the government of Benin could sustain the operations and maintenance of the project components. These steps included conducting a feasibility study, incorporating conditions precedent into the compact, hiring a port advisor, requiring a compact closure plan, and identifying steps the government of Benin should take to support sustainability in the compact letter of completion.

Feasibility study: In accordance with its policies, MCC funded a study to determine the technical and financial feasibility of the port activities proposed by the government of Benin. Through this process, MCC identified activities that would provide an economic benefit to Benin and ensure the likelihood for future sustainability.

Conditions precedent: Two conditions precedent were included in the compact to help ensure the sustainability of the port.

- First, the compact required the Port Authority to enter into a contract with a private firm to operate the new south wharf to ensure its open and transparent operation, eliminate corruption, and improve operations.
- Second, MCC required the Port of Cotonou to meet the International Ship and Port Facility Security code.[34] Meeting the code means that that ships stopping later at U.S. ports would not be required to undergo increased security scrutiny, thus decreasing costs to shipping companies.

Port advisor: MCC funded the hiring of a port advisor to review port operations and make recommendations to improve the operations of the port and ensure an adequate cash flow through increased shipping fees to operate the port. Compact closure plan: MCC requires all MCAs to create a Program Closure Plan, outlining the steps it will take when the compact ends to finalize any compact commitments in an orderly fashion. The Program Closure Plan for Benin includes some steps aimed at helping sustain the compact's investment, including for the Port of Cotonou. Most notably, the compact closure plan describes the government of Benin's intention to establish an agency, in part, to complete and implement a "MCA-Benin experience sustainability program."

Compact completion letter: MCC also sent a letter to the government of Benin in January 2012 to formally mark the conclusion of the compact and to provide final recommendations to ensure the sustainability of compact investments, among other things. In addition, MCC noted that efforts made by Benin to maximize the results and ensure the sustainability of this compact would be considered in decisions related to a potential second compact. The letter specifically identified the following as actions the government of Benin needs to complete:

- ensure the competitiveness of the Port of Cotonou and increase its throughput (including ensuring the fluidity of traffic through the port, implementing a suitable operations scheme for the truck parking facility, and controlling total fees charged to importers);
- complete customs department reforms;
- enforce port security systems (including control of truck and pedestrian access traffic); and
- execute the port channel access improvements required to meet the terms of the south wharf concession agreement and to achieve the intended increase in port capacity.

The Port Authority Has Been Unable to Operate Key Components of the Port, Calling into Question the Port's Long-Term Sustainability

Despite the steps MCC took to help ensure sustainability, several key port components were not operational at the end of the compact because the Port Authority had not taken the necessary steps to operate all project components (see table 3). The Port Authority's inability to operate all components of the port at compact completion calls into question its ability to maintain port operations and to achieve MCC's anticipated economic return.

Table 3. Status of Key Components of Port of Cotonou

Lot	Component	Status as of December 2011[a]	GAO findings	Status as of April 2012[b]	April 2012 updates
1	Jetty	●	Jetty is slowing the entry of sand into the port.	●	
2	South wharf	○	Concessionaire needs to install paving, cranes, and other infrastructure. Planned operational date: January 2013.	○	Port Authority has requested the International Finance Corporation to assist in findinga way to fund its commitment to dredge the port entry as required in the concession agreement.
3	East-west road	**○**	Congestion worse than before; 28 hours average truck-in-port-time versus 24 before compact.	**○**	Congestion still a problem.
	Security system	○	Lacks staff. Planned operational date: unknown.	**○**	Facilities turned over to the Port Authority in February 2012, about 10 staff in the control centers, in the process of hiring additional staff to operate the system, and identification badge system notin use.
	Electricity distribution system	**○**	Needs new increased power feed from local utility. Planned full operational date: unknown.	**○**	Waiting on increased power feed from local utility, but not expected before January 2013.
	Fire protection (station, trucks, and water tank)	○	Lacks staff, and traffic congestion prevents circulation of fire trucks. Planned full operational date: unknown.	**○**	Port Authority is using fire trucks, developing operation plan, increasing staff, recruiting staff, training staff,

Lot	Component	Status as of December 2011[a]	GAO findings	Status as of April 2012[b]	April 2012 updates
					and waiting for correction of construction defects to be fully operational.
	Weigh station	○	Under construction.	○	Construction complete, calibration of scales and training under way; plan is to be operational in June 2012.
	Lighting	●	In operation.	●	
3A	Bypass road	**O**	Parked trucks prevent one lane from being used.	**O**	Trucks still using one lane of road for parking.
	Railway	●	In operation.	●	
	Boundary wall	**O**	At least one breach in wall identified, gates need to be installed by concessionaire at south wharf site.	**O**	Gates not yet constructed by concessionaire.
	Truck parking lot	○	Lot not in use and no concessionaire hired to operate the lot. Planned operational date: unknown.	**O**	Port Authority plans to sign a concession agreement in July 2012, and Port Authority occasionally uses the lot.
	Lighting for parking lot	○	Lights not yet installed.	●	Lighting completed.

●: In operation.

O: In operation but not fully utilized.

○: Not in operation.

Source: GAO analysis of data from MCC, the Autonomous Port of Cotonou, Bolloré Africa Logistics, Maersk Line, and Royal Haskoning.

[a] GAO conducted a site inspection in December 2011.

[b] Update based on April 2012 correspondence with the construction supervisor, Port Authority, and port shipping companies.

South Wharf Is Not in Use

Although MCC funded a new south wharf to increase tonnage moving through the port, and ensured that the Port Authority contracted a concessionaire to operate the south wharf, to increase private investment and generate income for the Port Authority, it is not in operation because the Port Authority has not completed additional dredging and the concessionaire has not finished the landside works, such as paving the wharf area or installing cranes (see fig. 24).[35]

Figure 24. Constructed South Wharf without Landside Infrastructure.

In exchange for the right to manage and operate the south wharf, the concessionaire paid the Port Authority a concession fee. The Port Authority intended to use that fee to deepen the access channel—its contractual obligation under the agreement—so that larger cargo ships could use the concessionaire's facility. The concessionaire also agreed to construct or install the necessary landside equipment and infrastructure. However, because of an error in assessing the amount of work to be done and an underestimation of the cost, the concession fee was insufficient to fund the required dredging. A Port Authority official stated in April 2012 the Port Authority is currently evaluating bids for the work. The concession agreement also stipulated that the concession should be operational 18 months after the concession start date. However, according to a concessionaire official, the concession company had not yet agreed upon a start date with the Port Authority as of April 2012.[36] However, the concessionaire was proceeding with constructing its portion of the landside works. MCC officials stated that the concessionaire's construction will be completed in December 2012, and a concessionaire official told us the wharf would be operational in January 2013; however, if the Port Authority does not honor its part of the concession agreement and finish the dredging, a concessionaire official stated it may reduce the amount of landside works it is going to finish, such as not install as many cranes or not pave the entire wharf area, because it could operate the south wharf only for smaller ships. Smaller ships and reduced wharf area would likely reduce the amount of cargo tonnage through the port and the fees the port would receive from the concession. As of April 2012, the Port Authority had requested the International Finance Corporation's assistance investigating how it could fund the required dredging and meet its commitment of the concession agreement, but it had not yet awarded any contracts to perform the work.[37]

Security System Is Not Being Fully Utilized

The Port of Cotonou may be unable to provide effective security for the port or retain its International Ship and Port Facility Security certification because the MCC-funded port security system was not in operation as of our December 2011 visit.[38] The Port Authority had not hired sufficient staff, enforced its security policies, or maintained its security perimeter.

- The security system requires 150 to 257 individuals to staff the operations on a 24-hour basis. [39] As of April 2012, there were about 90 security personnel on staff and, according to a port authority official, the port authority was recruiting an additional 25 people. The construction supervisor stated that as of April 2012 the Port Authority had about 10 individuals staffing only the operation of two control and surveillance centers, which, according to MCC officials, were being operated only during the day. Without adequate trained staff, the security system cannot function to its full capacity.
- The Port Authority was not fully enforcing established security policies, as of December 2011. For example, the port was not fully controlling access to the port. Even though a Port Authority official stated that everyone entering the port is required to wear some form of identification (a badge, arm bracelet, or uniform), in our December 2011 site visit we observed several visitors with improper or no identification at all. According to a Port Authority official, the MCC-funded access system was still not in full operation as of April 2012.
- In December 2011, we also observed a railway access gate had not been installed on the south wharf site, creating a breach in the boundary wall allowing people to bypass the security system and gain entry into the port. The gate was not a part of the MCC-funded work,

and while the Port Authority is working with the wharf concessionaire to install a gate at the location, the temporary measure implemented by the Port Authority leaves the port vulnerable (see fig. 25).

Source: GAO.

Figure 25. Breach in Boundary Wall.

Electricity Distribution System Lacks Sufficient Power to Operate at Capacity

MCC funded an electricity distribution system for the port that does not function to capacity because the Port Authority had not ensured that the amount of power transmitted to the port from the power company would be adequate. The MCC-funded distribution system was designed to distribute 15 megavolt-amps of electricity and planned to initially provide 10 megavolt-amps; however, the current conduit to the port provides only 2 megavolt-amps. Until the 10 megavolt-amps of power is provided, the contractor cannot make final connections or test the system. As of April 2012, a project management official reported that the increased power service had not yet been provided to the system and the officials did not expect it to be provided before the October 2012 end of the defects liability period. That same month MCC officials told us that they did not expect the power service to be upgraded before January 2013.

Fire Station Lacked Sufficient Staff to Operate MCC-Funded Fire Engines

The MCC-funded fire station was not in use as of December 2011 because the Port Authority had not hired sufficient staff. The Port Authority received three new fire engines as part of the MCC project, but had not increased the staffing level, which MCA-Benin's feasibility study stated was necessary to operate the fire engines on a 24-hour basis. In addition, truck congestion on the roads within the port prevents the fire engines from circulating when needed.

As of April 2012, port authority officials stated that the fire protection system was still not in service because of construction defects in the water tank valve and testing had not been completed. However, the port officials stated that they had recruited and trained additional firemen, and were recruiting other personnel to operate and maintain the system, such as inspectors, a diesel mechanic, and plumbers. At the time of the feasibility study, the Port Authority had 14 fire prevention staff. In April 2012, a Port Authority official stated that the authority plans for a total staff of 25.

Port Roads Are Severely Congested

Although the east-west port road and the bypass road were completed with only minor quality issues such as missing manhole covers, significant truck congestion jeopardizes their utility. The compact goal was to reduce the average number of hours trucks stayed at the port from 24 hours to 7 hours. However, the average after the compact ended is 28 hours. According to officials from two shipping companies, one of their primary concerns was that truck congestion at the port would likely limit their ability to increase the volume of merchandise passing through the port (see fig. 26).

The Port Authority has taken some steps to alleviate the truck congestion. For example, the Benin government engaged a private firm to install tracking and communication devices in trucks beginning in December 2011 that would allow trucks to enter the port when their shipper is ready to load or unload them. However, an official from the firm stated that, as of April 2012, the Benin government had not allowed the firm to initiate the system even though it has been ready to operate since late November 2011. The government of Benin also has plans to move some operations to off-site "dry ports" where containers will go through customs and be loaded and emptied. However, shipping company officials questioned whether the existing railway will be able to transfer the cargo to the dry ports. According to March 2012 statements by shipping company officials, the Port Authority attempted to implement the use of the railway and a privately operated dry port for containers going to hinterland countries at a site about 55 kilometers away from the port.[40] However, according to one of the shipping company officials, the railway could transport only 90 of the 200 containers needed to be transported daily to the dry port. One shipping company official stated the company had over 1,700 containers backlogged in the port in early March 2012, taking an average of more than 25 days to get a container from the port to the dry port. Shipping officials reported that as of late March 2012, port officials have allowed the containers to be either loaded and emptied in the port or transported by truck to another dry port, but congestion was still a problem.

Source: GAO.

Figure 26. Congestion on the East-West Port Road.

Parking Lot in Operation but Not Being Fully Utilized

MCC funded the construction of a 250-truck parking lot that was handed over to the Port Authority in September 2011; however, as of April 2012, Port Authority officials stated the parking lot was not in full use because they had not engaged a company to manage the concession. MCC officials stated that trucks are occasionally moved to the lot to alleviate congestion. Port Authority officials stated that they plan to sign a concession agreement In July 2012 to manage the lot.

CONCLUSION

Some of the challenges MCC faced in Georgia and Benin were not unique. As with other early compacts, insufficient planning, escalation of construction costs, and insufficient MCC review led to project delays, scope changes, and cost increases. In the case of Georgia, MCC specifically had problems ensuring the quality of its transportation infrastructure project even though it had a quality assurance framework because it did not adequately address problems in contract supervision identified by the independent engineer. As a result, the road had significant pavement defects and numerous quality issues at compact completion. Furthermore, MCC has no leverage over the government or contractors once compacts end, even though contractors may be expected to continue work in the 1-year defects liability period following the contract. In Georgia, the construction contractors were required to remediate quality issues after the end of the contract, but MCC cannot at this point ensure that the repair work is properly done.

Even though MCC took steps to provide for the sustainability of its investments in both Georgia and Benin, the projects in both countries have maintenance and operability challenges that jeopardize the benefits they were projected to achieve. In Georgia, the ability of the government to maintain the road is in question. Without sustained maintenance—such as repairing drainage systems and removing snow—the road will need additional repairs and have limited usefulness in the winter. In Benin, key project components, including security and electricity distribution systems and the south wharf, were not operational at the end of the compact. The operation of these and other interconnected systems depends on the partner government, which to date has been unable to fund and implement the work required to begin port operations. As a result, MCC may have invested considerable U.S. resources in equipment and structures that will not be used to maximum benefit and thus not provide the expected economic benefits. MCC should take this opportunity to review the problems that emerged from Georgia, Benin, and other completed compacts and to establish or strengthen mechanisms by which it can better invest U.S. resources in future compacts.

Recommendations for Executive Action

To maximize the quality and sustainability of future projects, we recommend that the MCC Chief Executive Officer take the following actions:

To ensure that its quality assurance framework is fully implemented and to ensure that transportation infrastructure projects are built to the established quality standards, MCC should

- review how MCC uses information and professional recommendations provided by its independent engineers to address identified deficiencies and to ensure projects are constructed to the quality standards set out in contracts, and
- develop a mechanism to maintain influence through contracts' defects liability periods when they extend beyond the compact end date.

To ensure sustainability of compact projects, MCC should evaluate the effectiveness of the tools it uses (such as its feasibility studies and conditions precedent) to ensure that partner countries have adequate infrastructure, staff, and policies necessary to operate and maintain MCC-funded infrastructure following the compact.

AGENCY COMMENTS AND OUR EVALUATION

In written comments on a draft of this report, MCC stated that it agrees with our three recommendations; however, it did not commit to undertaking any specific actions to address them. With respect to the first recommendation to review its use of information and recommendations from its independent engineers, MCC stated that it does guide its oversight of compact projects using the analysis provided by its independent engineers, but that the quality of advice can vary and independent engineers are not always privy to all factors affecting compact programs.

However, MCC did not state that it would review its practices regarding how it uses information from these independent engineers. With respect to our second recommendation regarding the need for a mechanism to maintain influence on contracts whose defects liability periods extend beyond compact end dates, MCC noted that it sustains a dialogue with its partner countries after compact closure to emphasize the importance of continued oversight. However, as MCC officials have noted, because its authorizing legislation limits the term of compacts to 5 years, MCC's ability to assist partner countries directly once a compact closes is restricted. MCC did not state that it would seek any additional authority to maintain influence after the end of a compact.

With respect to our third recommendation, to evaluate the tools it uses to ensure projects' sustainability, MCC listed ways that it works to ensure sustainability throughout the development, implementation, and closure of compact programs.

MCC also noted that it revised its Compact Development Guidelines in January 2012 and included steps to strengthen the agency's assessment of sustainability during compact development. However, MCC did not commit to evaluate the effectiveness of the tools it has used or plans to use to ensure its projects' sustainability.

We incorporated technical comments from MCC in our report where appropriate.

David Gootnick
Director
International Affairs and Trade

APPENDIX I: OBJECTIVES, SCOPE, AND METHODOLOGY

The fiscal year 2008 Consolidated Appropriations Act, Public Law 110-161, mandated that GAO review the results of Millennium Challenge Corporation's (MCC) compacts.

For the purpose of this engagement, we examined the quality and sustainability of MCC's two transportation infrastructure projects in Georgia (the Samtskhe-Javakheti Road Rehabilitation Activity) and Benin (the Port of Cotonou Access to Markets Project). Transportation infrastructure is defined as public works that provide the conveyance of passengers or goods from one place to another.

GAO selected MCC's compacts in Georgia and Benin as the focus of this engagement through a subjective process. Our selection universe was those compacts ending in 2010 and 2011 that had a transportation infrastructure project.

In a previous engagement we had reviewed the MCC-funded transportation infrastructure projects in Cape Verde and Honduras.[1] Georgia and Benin, in combination with these previously reviewed projects, provided some geographic variety as well as the ability to compare two port projects and two large road projects.

We based our assessment of the projects' quality on the quality assurance requirements established by MCC, the partner countries' Millennium Challenge Accounts (MCA), and their contractors. MCC requires the MCAs to (1) have an individual project director or to engage the services of a project management firm to help manage the administrative aspects of compact programs, (2) contract with implementing partners (such as construction firms) using MCC's procurement guidelines, and (3) engage a construction supervisor to oversee the day-to-day construction and ensure compliance with contract requirements.

For this report, the definition of sustainability is based on the definition from the Organisation for Economic Cooperation and Development's Development Assistance Committee, which defines "sustainability" as "the continuation of benefits from a development intervention after major development assistance has been completed."

The Organisation for Economic Cooperation and Development's Development Assistance Committee is an international forum of many of the largest funders of aid with a mandate to promote development cooperation and other policies so as to contribute to sustainable development. We operationalized this definition by specifying that sustainability is the ability of MCC's partner country governments to operate and maintain the new infrastructure in such a condition as is required to produce the projected benefits for the period of time those benefits are calculated.

To assess the quality and longer-term sustainability for compacts in Georgia and Benin, we analyzed MCC, MCA, and other documents; interviewed MCC officials and stakeholders; and observed project results in both countries.

- We reviewed the compact agreement for Georgia and Benin. We also reviewed documents prepared by MCA officials, independent construction supervisors, project management consultants, MCC independent engineers, and government officials, including monthly reports, special studies, testing reports, and daily inspections. We also reviewed final reports submitted to MCA by contractors on compact activities.
- We interviewed MCC and MCA officials in both countries regarding the results of each compact activity, including the quality and sustainability of the projects. We visited infrastructure projects in both countries, including visits to the port in Benin, and to the Samtskhe-Javakheti road in Georgia. We met with project construction contractors, independent construction supervisors, and MCA project management consultants. In addition, we interviewed officials from the governments of Georgia and Benin about compact implementation, results, and sustainability, including Benin's Ministry of Maritime Economy and Port Authority, and Georgia's Ministry of Infrastructure.

- We traveled to Benin and the Republic of Georgia in December 2011 and conducted site inspections to verify the extent to which the MCC-funded transportation infrastructure projects had been completed and to observe whether there were any visible deficiencies in construction. All photographs in this report attributed to GAO were taken during this time period.

These interviews, document reviews, and site visits were used to determine if the MCAs had implemented MCC's quality assurance framework, if there was supporting documentation to verify that quality testing had been undertaken, if any quality deficiencies were encountered during construction, if any quality deficiencies remain, and whether the infrastructure projects would be sustainable. We were not able to view actual work in progress or visit testing facilities for most infrastructure contracts because the work had already been completed.

To determine the amount of funding used for transportation infrastructure projects, we reviewed MCC financial data. We included compact implementation funding—funds disbursed before entry into force to facilitate the implementation of the compact—with other projects not related to transportation infrastructure.

MCC enters into a legal relationship with partner country governments, which vest responsibility for day-to-day management of compact project implementation in the MCA, including monitoring and evaluation activities such as setting and revising targets, but such MCA actions require MCC's direct oversight and approval. Therefore, throughout this report, we attribute all decisions related to project rescoping and compact targets to MCC.

Finally, some of the reports and documents referenced above were written in French or Georgian. We translated these documents internally to enable our analysis.

We conducted this performance audit from November 2011 to June 2012 in accordance with generally accepted government auditing standards. Those standards require that we plan and perform the audit to obtain sufficient, appropriate evidence to provide a reasonable basis for our findings and conclusions based on our audit objectives. We believe the evidence obtained provides a reasonable basis for our findings and conclusions based on our audit objectives.

Appendix II: Additional Photographs Related to Figure 20: Compact-Funded Improvements in the Port of Cotonou

The following photographs illustrate various components of the MCC-funded Port of Cotonou project in Benin. For a map of the port, which indicates where these components are located, see figure 20.

Source: GAO.

End Notes

[1] 22 U.S.C. § 7708(j).

[2] MCC commits funding when a compact is signed and obligates funds after the compact enters into force. As of June 2012, MCC had signed initial compacts with, in order of signature, Madagascar, Honduras, Cape Verde, Nicaragua, Georgia, Benin, Vanuatu, Armenia, Ghana, Mali, El Salvador, Mozambique, Lesotho, Morocco, Mongolia, Tanzania, Burkina Faso, Namibia, Senegal, Moldova, the Philippines, Jordan, Malawi, Indonesia and Zambia. In February 2012, MCC signed a second compact with Cape Verde.

[3] Consolidated Appropriations Act, 2008, Pub. L. No. 110-161, § 668(d)(1)(A). The act also required us to examine the financial control and procurement practices of MCC and its

accountable entities. We responded to this requirement separately in GAO, *Millennium Challenge Corporation: MCC Has Addressed a Number of Implementation Challenges, but Needs to Improve Financial Controls and Infrastructure Planning*, GAO-10-52 (Washington, D.C.: Nov. 6, 2009).

[4] The 5 other completed compacts are Honduras, Cape Verde, Nicaragua, Vanuatu, and Armenia. We do not include the Madagascar compact in this list of compacts because, as the result of a pattern of actions inconsistent with MCC policy, MCC formally terminated the compact effective August 31, 2009. Protests and instability in Madagascar in January 2009 ultimately led to the forced resignation of the country's elected president.

[5] See GAO-10-52 and GAO, *Millennium Challenge Corporation: Compacts in Cape Verde and Honduras Achieved Reduced Targets,* GAO-11-728 (Washington, D.C.: July 27, 2011). In GAO-10-52, GAO recommended that MCC should (1) establish a programmatic goal that MCAs conclude all project planning efforts—to include MCC final approvals of the MCAs' final feasibility surveys, engineering surveys, environmental surveys, and resettlement studies—prior to entry into force, but not later than the point at which the MCAs issue contract solicitations; and (2) require MCAs to obtain detailed reviews of project cost estimates—to include the extent that risks to projects, such as cost escalation, schedule delays, and other issues, have been considered—and of project designs before contract solicitation for large construction projects to better ensure that projects can be successfully bid and built. In GAO-11-728, GAO recommended that MCC should work with partner countries to make project planning, design, and construction decisions that reduce long-term maintenance needs and costs to maximize the sustainability of MCC-funded infrastructure projects and reduce the amount of maintenance required after compact completion.

[6] Partner country governments vest responsibility for day-to-day management of MCC compact project implementation in accountable entities, usually referred to as Millennium Challenge Accounts.

[7] Other board members are the U.S. Trade Representative, the Administrator of the U.S. Agency for International Development, the CEO of MCC, and up to four Senate-confirmed nongovernmental members appointed by the President from lists of individuals submitted by congressional leadership.

[8] The organization of the management structure may vary across compacts and projects.

[9] Testing is typically completed to ensure construction materials meet performance characteristics. For example, compaction tests are done to ensure underlying soils can support pavement structures. In addition, completed work is tested to ensure that it was installed properly and performs as intended. For example, smoothness tests are performed on newly placed pavements.

[10] In essence, "substantially complete" means that the works can generally be used as intended and that only minor work remains.

[11] The number of kilometers of road rehabilitated (217) is based on GAO's review of MCC provided takeover certificates indicating the number of kilometers of road accepted from the construction contractors as complete and a March 2012 trip report issued by MCC's independent engineer. In some documents, MCC reports rehabilitating 220 kilometers of road, including sections of the road where small amounts of finishing work (e.g. painting) were undertaken even through major road works were not done on those sections.

[12] Actual construction began in the town of Teleti, at the outskirts of Tbilisi.

[13] Each section of road to be constructed in Georgia is described as a lot. The lots include construction works such as pavement rehabilitation, bridge rehabilitation or replacement, drainage systems, guardrails and concrete barrier walls, signage, and pavement markings.

MCA-Georgia named the lots as follows: 1, 2, 3, 3A, 4, 5i, 5ii, 6i, 6ii, 6iii, and 7. We have used its nomenclature.

[14] As of our December 2011 site visit, the border crossing with Turkey was not open because the Turkish government had not yet installed the necessary infrastructure on its side of the border. The government of Georgia anticipates its opening in 2013.

[15] For additional information on the projects included in the Georgia Compact, see GAO, *Millennium Challenge Corporation: Summary Fact Sheets for 17 Compacts,* GAO-10-797R (Washington, D.C.: July 14, 2010).

[16] Funds were transferred from the regional infrastructure development project, energy rehabilitation project, Georgia regional development fund project, agribusiness development project, program administration, audit, and fiscal and procurement management activities.

[17] GAO discussed these initial cost escalation and planning challenges in a previous report. See GAO-10-52.

[18] Lot 6iii was added as an addendum to the contract for lot 6ii in August 2009.

[19] A contractor's quality assurance plan identifies such things as the type of tests to be conducted, the frequency at which materials will be tested, and how the results will be reported.

[20] MCC stated the value of the construction supervisor's contract increased from an initial value of $2.7 million to a final value of $7.4 million.

[21] The independent engineer reported that the firm's fee was 3.5 percent of the contract cost, while the international norm is 5 to 6 percent. According to MCC, MCA-Georgia spent a total of 4.2 percent of the overall construction costs on supervision of all road lots.

[22] MCC reports indicated an average International Roughness Index (IRI) of 16.6 before the rehabilitation and 1.5 after the rehabilitation. IRI is a measure of road pavement roughness in terms of meters per kilometer. The IRI affects vehicle operating costs, ride quality, and road damage.

[23] We found noticeable pavement deterioration and repairs in lots 2, 3, 3A, 4, and 6ii.

[24] We received an update from the construction supervisor of the construction defects remaining as of March 2012, but the reporting format is not the same as used at the time of takeover, and as a result, it is not possible to evaluate how many of those defects remain or new defects have appeared.

[25] These performance guarantees are contractual instruments with a third party that allow the Georgian government to ensure a contractor meets its contractual obligations or the Georgian government can have the third party pay to complete the contractors' commitments, up to the amount of the guarantee.

[26] The MCC independent engineer reported in March 2012 that it expected final acceptance of lots 1, 4, 6ii, and 6iii in April 2012—about 3 to 4 months after the end of their 1-year defects liability periods and final acceptance of lots 2, 3, 3A, 5i, 5ii, 6i, and 7 in July 2012—about 4 to 8 months after the end of their defects liability periods.

[27] User costs include such items as vehicle maintenance, tire wear, increased fuel and oil costs, and vehicle depreciation.

[28] "Conditions precedent" are terms in an agreement that indicate that certain conditions must be met by one party before a second party to the contract is obligated to perform or do its part. In the case of an MCC compact, MCC establishes conditions precedent that must be met by the partner government or MCA before MCC disburses funds.

[29] According to MCC, the funding requirements set out as the condition precedent were for the entire Georgian road network and not just for the MCC-funded road.

[30] In its response to a draft of this report, MCC again stated that the government of Georgia has communicated its commitment to ensuring the defects are fixed and to maintain the road over the long term. See appendix III.

[31] For additional information on the projects included in the Benin compact, see GAO-10-797R.

[32] Additional dredging is required to accommodate larger ships as set out in the conditions of the concession agreement negotiated by the Port Authority for a private firm to operate the new south wharf.

[33] In technical comments on a draft of this report, MCC noted that MCA-Benin's works contracts were based on the FIDIC yellow book, pursuant to which a third-party engineer, hired by MCA-Benin, was contractually responsible for determining when the works had achieved substantial completion. MCC also noted that all but 5 have been remediated.

[34] The International Ship and Port Facility Security (ISPS) code is a comprehensive set of measures to enhance the security of ships and port facilities. The purpose of the ISPS code is to provide a standardized, consistent framework for evaluating risk, enabling governments to offset changes in threat with changes in vulnerability for ships and port facilities through determination of appropriate security levels and corresponding security measures. The ISPS code is implemented through chapter XI-2 special measures to enhance maritime security in the International Convention for the Safety of Life at Sea (SOLAS), 1974.

[35] In technical comments provided by MCC on a draft of this report, MCC stated that there was never an expectation that all landside works required to operate the new south wharf at full capacity would be completed by the end of the compact term (October 2011). However, the economic analysis prepared for MCC's investment decision in 2005 shows that the expansion of shipping capacity due to the South Wharf investment would be fully available in 2010.

[36] In its initial economic rate of return analysis, MCC had anticipated that, by 2010, the south wharf would have increased the capacity of the port by almost 30 percent.

[37] The International Finance Corporation is a member of the World Bank Group.

[38] The new security system was turned over to the Port Authority in February 2012 and includes a control and surveillance center, a secondary control and surveillance center, a visitors' reception center to issue badges, six access control stations, perimeter fencing with port intrusion detection, security cameras, alarms, radio communications, and computer equipment to operate it.

[39] The port authority estimated 150 security personnel are required to operate the new security system, while the contractor installing the system calculated about 192 security personnel are required to operate the system 24 hours a day, 7 days a week, and the project management consultant for the project calculated 257 security personnel were required to adequately secure the port 24 hours per day.

[40] Hinterland countries are those inland countries that lie behind a port. For Benin, the hinterland countries include Niger, Burkina Faso, Chad, and Mali. Togo and Nigeria are also common destinations for goods transiting through the Port of Cotonou.

End Notes for Appendix I

[1] GAO, *Millennium Challenge Corporation: Compacts in Cape Verde and Honduras Achieved Reduced Targets,* GAO-11-728 (Washington, D.C.: July 25, 2011).

INDEX

N

O

P

Q

R

S

T

U

V

W